Robert Cooke

The Visitation of London in the Year 1568

Salzwasser

Robert Cooke

The Visitation of London in the Year 1568

1. Auflage | ISBN: 978-3-84605-082-8

Erscheinungsort: Frankfurt, Deutschland

Erscheinungsjahr: 2020

Salzwasser Verlag GmbH

Reprint of the original, first published in 1869.

THE

PUBLICATIONS

OF

The Harleian Society.

ESTABLISHED A.D. MDCCCLXIX.

Volume I.

FOR THE YEAR MDCCCLXIX.

TAYLOR AND CO., PRINTERS,
LITTLE QUEEN STREET, LINCOLN'S INN FIELDS.

The Visitation of London

In the Year

1568.

TAKEN BY

R O B E R T   C O O K E,

Clarenceux King of Arms,

AND SINCE AUGMENTED BOTH WITH DESCENTS AND ARMS.

EDITED BY

JOSEPH JACKSON HOWARD, LL.D., F.S.A.,

AND

GEORGE JOHN ARMYTAGE, F.S.A.

At a Meeting of the Council of the HARLEIAN SOCIETY, *held at 8, Danes Inn, London, W.C., on the 28th day of May,* 1869, *the Honourable* HENRY ROPER CURZON *in the Chair, it was resolved that—*

"*The First Publication of the Society be* THE HERALDIC VISITATION OF LONDON IN 1568, *by Robert Cooke, Clarenceux King of Arms, to be edited by* JOSEPH JACKSON HOWARD, ESQ., LL.D., F.S.A., *and* GEORGE JOHN ARMYTAGE, ESQ., F.S.A."

Preface.

———◆———

THE Visitation contained in the following pages was taken by Robert Cooke, Clarenceux King of Arms in the year 1568. The copy from which it is transcribed forms one of the Harleian Manuscripts in the British Museum. It is in the handwriting of Nicholas Charles, who died in 1613, and the additions subsequent to that date are by William Camden, Clarenceux King of Arms, who bought Charles's books at his death. It is impossible to draw the exact line between the original Visitation and the additions, but the undoubted repute in which both heralds were held who possessed it renders it unnecessary.

The Editors cannot conclude these few preliminary remarks without acknowledging their great obligation to Mr. JOHN DAVIDSON, a member of the Council of the Harleian Society, to whom the Society is indebted for the very elaborate Index appended to the Work.

JOSEPH JACKSON HOWARD.
GEORGE J. ARMYTAGE.

LONDON,
   December 31st, 1869.

List of Pedigrees.

The Visitacon of London,

TAKEN BY ROBERT COOKE, CLARENCEUX KING OF ARMES, ANº DOM. 1568, AND SINCE AUGMENTED BOTH WITH DESCENTS AND ARMES. (HARL. MSS., No. 1463.)

Chester.

ARMS. *Per pale argent and sable, a chevron engrailed between three rams'-heads erased, armed or, all counterchanged, within a bordure engrailed gules bezanté.*
CREST. *A ram's-head couped argent, armed or.*

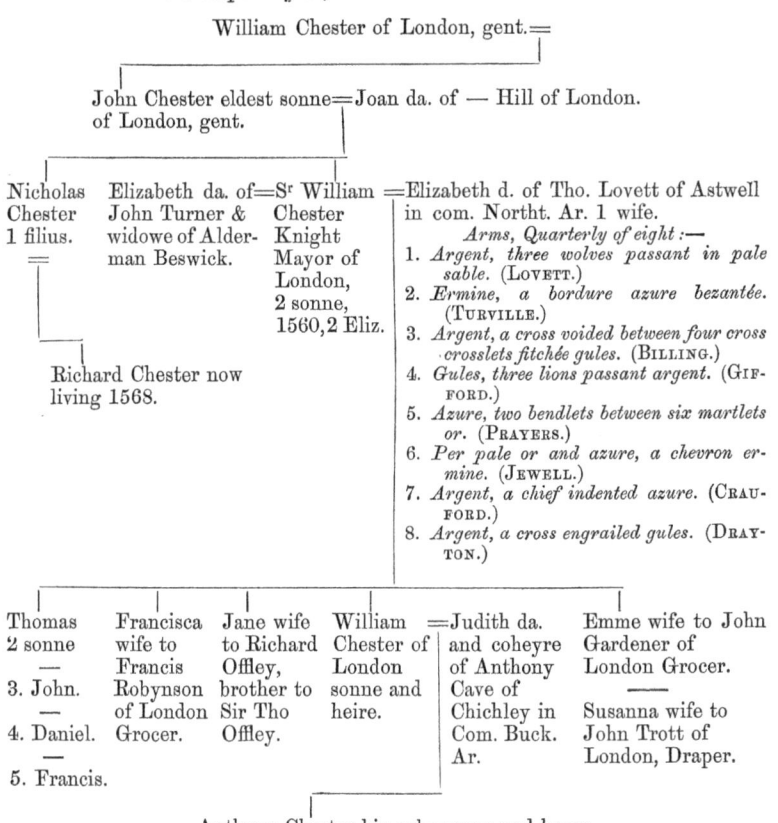

William Chester of London, gent.⹀

John Chester eldest sonne⹀Joan da. of — Hill of London.
of London, gent.

Nicholas Chester 1 filius.⹀

Elizabeth da. of John Turner & widowe of Alderman Beswick.

Sʳ William Chester Knight Mayor of London, 2 sonne, 1560,2 Eliz.⹀Elizabeth d. of Tho. Lovett of Astwell in com. Northt. Ar. 1 wife.

Arms, Quarterly of eight :—
1. *Argent, three wolves passant in pale sable.* (LOVETT.)
2. *Ermine, a bordure azure bezantée.* (TURVILLE.)
3. *Argent, a cross voided between four cross crosslets fitchée gules.* (BILLING.)
4. *Gules, three lions passant argent.* (GIFFORD.)
5. *Azure, two bendlets between six martlets or.* (PRAYERS.)
6. *Per pale or and azure, a chevron ermine.* (JEWELL.)
7. *Argent, a chief indented azure.* (CRAUFORD.)
8. *Argent, a cross engrailed gules.* (DRAYTON.)

Richard Chester now living 1568.

Thomas 2 sonne — 3. John. — 4. Daniel. — 5. Francis.

Francisca wife to Francis Robynson of London Grocer.

Jane wife to Richard Offley, brother to Sir Tho Offley.

William Chester of London sonne and heire.⹀Judith da. and coheyre of Anthony Cave of Chichley in Com. Buck. Ar.

Emme wife to John Gardener of London Grocer.

Susanna wife to John Trott of London, Draper.

Anthony Chester his only sonne and heyre.

B

𝕯𝖍𝖎𝖙𝖊.

ARMS. *Per fess azure and or, a pale counterchanged, upon the first three plates each charged with two bars wavy vert, on the second as many lions' heads erased gules.*
CREST. *A lion's head erased quarterly azure and or, gutté counterchanged.*

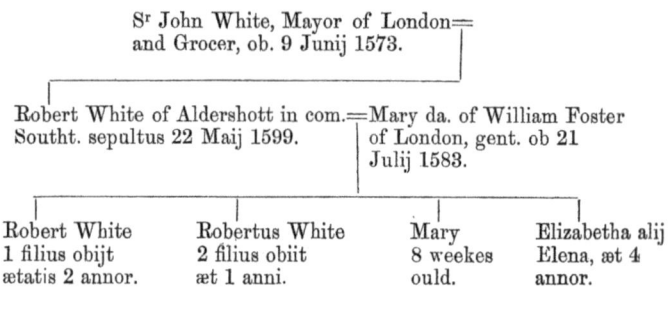

Sᵣ John White, Mayor of London
and Grocer, ob. 9 Junij 1573.

Robert White of Aldershott in com. = Mary da. of William Foster
Southt. sepultus 22 Maij 1599.   of London, gent. ob 21
                                                    Julij 1583.

| Robert White 1 filius obijt ætatis 2 annor. | Robertus White 2 filius obiit æt 1 anni. | Mary 8 weekes ould. | Elizabetha alij Elena, æt 4 annor. |

𝕸𝖆𝖗𝖙𝖞𝖓.

ARMS. *Quarterly :—1 and 4. Argent, a chevron between three mascles sable within a bordure engrailed gules.   2 and 3. Gules, a fess engrailed between three swans' heads erased argent (both for* MARTYN*).*
CREST. *A cockatrice's head or, beaked and wattled gules, between two wings expanded vert.*

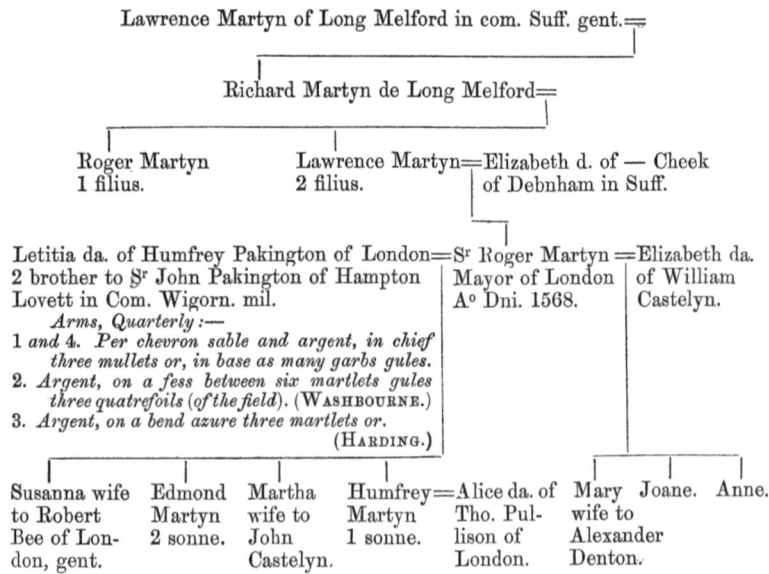

Lawrence Martyn of Long Melford in com. Suff. gent. =

Richard Martyn de Long Melford =

| Roger Martyn 1 filius. | Lawrence Martyn = Elizabeth d. of — Cheek 2 filius.   of Debnham in Suff. |

Letitia da. of Humfrey Pakington of London = Sᵣ Roger Martyn = Elizabeth da.
2 brother to Sᵣ John Pakington of Hampton   Mayor of London   of William
Lovett in Com. Wigorn. mil.   Aᵒ Dni. 1568.   Castelyn.
   Arms, Quarterly :—
1 *and* 4. *Per chevron sable and argent, in chief*
      three mullets or, in base as many garbs gules.
2. *Argent, on a fess between six martlets gules*
      three quatrefoils (of the field). (WASHBOURNE.)
3. *Argent, on a bend azure three martlets or.*
                                        (HARDING.)

| Susanna wife to Robert Bee of London, gent. | Edmond Martyn 2 sonne. | Martha wife to John Castelyn. | Humfrey Martyn 1 sonne. | = Alice da. of Tho. Pullison of London. | Mary wife to Alexander Denton. | Joane. | Anne. |

Champion.

ARMS. *Or, on a fess gules between three trefoils slipped ermines, an eagle displayed of the field within a bordure engrailed azure.*
CREST. *An arm erect couped at the elbow, habited gules, charged with three bars or, holding in the hand proper a rose-branch of the last.*

Sᵣ Richard Champion=Barbara da. of — Watson of Lidington in com.
Knight, Mayor of   Rotel gen.
London, Aᵒ Dni 1565.   ARMS. *Argent, on a chevron engrailed azure between three martlets sable as many crescents or, each charged with a torteau.*

Abenon.

ARMS. *Ermine, on a pale gules a cross flory or, on a chief sable a billet of the third within a mascle between two escallops argent.*
CREST. *A parrot's head erased vert, wings expanded per pale azure and gules, double collared or, holding in his beak of the third an olive-branch of the first.*

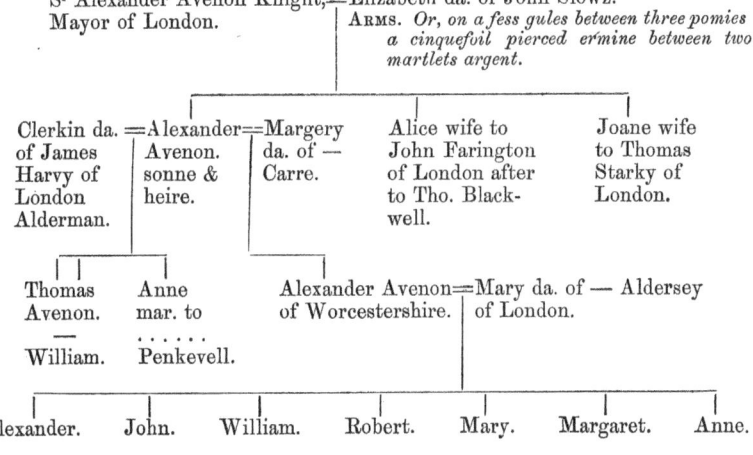

Sᵣ Alexander Avenon Knight,=Elizabeth da. of John Slowz.
Mayor of London.   ARMS. *Or, on a fess gules between three pomies a cinquefoil pierced ermine between two martlets argent.*

Clerkin da. =Alexander==Margery   Alice wife to   Joane wife
of James   Avenon.   da. of — John Farington to Thomas
Harvy of   sonne &   Carre.   of London after Starky of
London   heire.   to Tho. Black- London.
Alderman.   well.

Thomas   Anne   Alexander Avenon=Mary da. of — Aldersey
Avenon.   mar. to of Worcestershire. of London.
—   . . . . . .
William. Penkevell.

Alexander. John. William. Robert. Mary. Margaret. Anne.

Harper.

ARMS. *Azure, on a fess between three eagles displayed or, a fret between two martlets of the first.*

CREST. *Upon a crescent or, charged with a fret between two martlets azure, an eagle displayed of the last.*

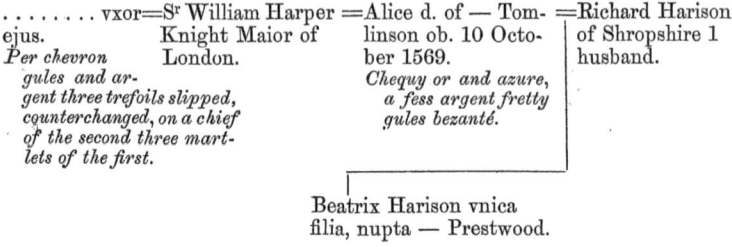

.... vxor=Sʳ William Harper =Alice d. of — Tom- =Richard Harison
ejus.　　　　　Knight Maior of　linson ob. 10 Octo-　of Shropshire 1
Per chevron　London.　　　　ber 1569.　　　　husband.
　gules and ar-　　　　　　　*Chequy or and azure,*
　gent three trefoils slipped,　　*a fess argent fretty*
　counterchanged, on a chief　　*gules bezanté.*
　of the second three mart-
　lets of the first.

Beatrix Harison vnica
filia, nupta — Prestwood.

Draper.

ARMS. *Quarterly:—1. Argent, on a fess between three annulets gules a mullet between two covered cups or* (DRAPER). *2. Argent, on two chevrons between three escallops sable six martlets or* (DRAPER). *3. Ermine, on a chief azure three lions rampant or* (AUCHER). *4. Ermine, a fess chequy sable and argent.* (URSWICK.)

CREST. *A stag's-head sable attired or, charged on the neck with two bars between three annulets of the second; a mullet for difference.*

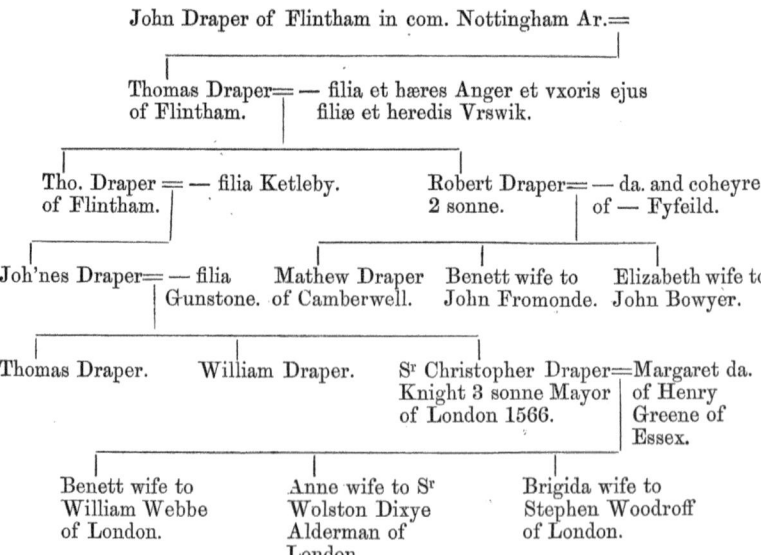

John Draper of Flintham in com. Nottingham Ar.=

Thomas Draper= — filia et hæres Anger et vxoris ejus
of Flintham.　　filiæ et heredis Vrswik.

Tho. Draper = — filia Ketleby.　　　Robert Draper= — da. and coheyre
of Flintham.　　　　　　　　　　2 sonne.　　　of — Fyfeild.

Joh'nes Draper= — filia　Mathew Draper　Benett wife to　Elizabeth wife to
　　　　Gunstone.　of Camberwell.　John Fromonde.　John Bowyer.

Thomas Draper.　　William Draper.　　Sʳ Christopher Draper=Margaret da.
　　　　　　　　　　　　　　　Knight 3 sonne Mayor　of Henry
　　　　　　　　　　　　　　　of London 1566.　　Greene of
　　　　　　　　　　　　　　　　　　　　Essex.

Benett wife to　　　Anne wife to Sʳ　　Brigida wife to
William Webbe　　Wolston Dixye　　Stephen Woodroff
of London.　　　Alderman of　　　of London.
　　　　　　　London.

Rowe.

ARMS. *Argent, on a chevron azure between three trefoils slipped party per pale gules and vert, three bezants ; in chief a crescent for difference.*
CREST. *Gules, a stag's-head attired or, a crescent for difference.*

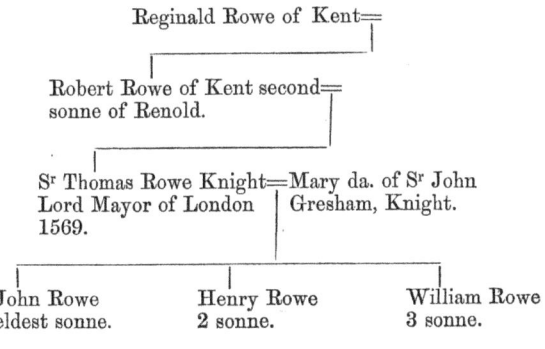

Reginald Rowe of Kent=

Robert Rowe of Kent second= sonne of Renold.

Sᵣ Thomas Rowe Knight=Mary da. of Sᵣ John Lord Mayor of London | Gresham, Knight. 1569.

John Rowe eldest sonne.

Henry Rowe 2 sonne.

William Rowe 3 sonne.

Garrard.

ARMS. *Argent, on a fess sable a lion passant of the field.*
CREST. *A leopard sejant proper.*

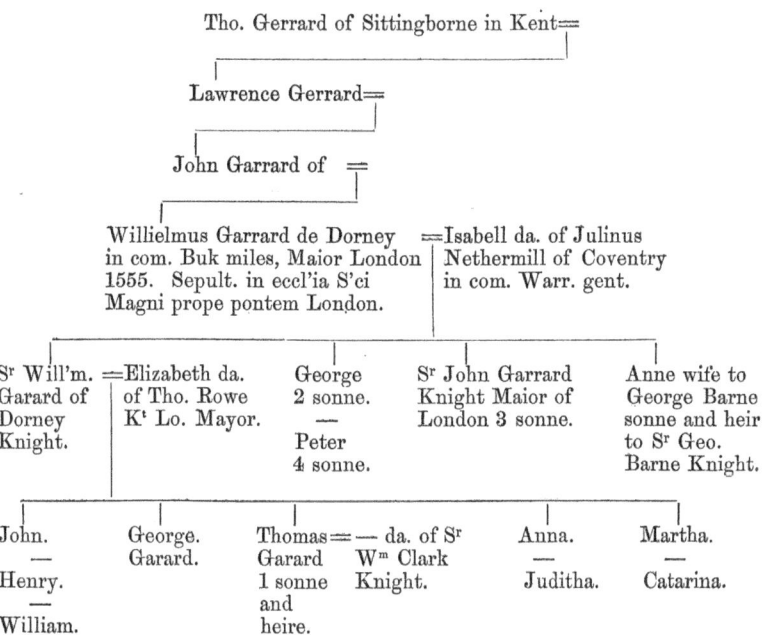

Tho. Gerrard of Sittingborne in Kent=

Lawrence Gerrard=

John Garrard of =

Willielmus Garrard de Dorney in com. Buk miles, Maior London 1555. Sepult. in eccl'ia S'ci Magni prope pontem London.

=Isabell da. of Julinus Nethermill of Coventry in com. Warr. gent.

Sᵣ Will'm. =Elizabeth da. Garard of | of Tho. Rowe Dorney | Kᵗ Lo. Mayor. Knight.

George 2 sonne. — Peter 4 sonne.

Sᵣ John Garrard Knight Maior of London 3 sonne.

Anne wife to George Barne sonne and heir to Sᵣ Geo. Barne Knight.

John. — Henry. — William.

George. Garard.

Thomas= — da. of Sᵣ Garard Wᵐ Clark 1 sonne Knight. and heire.

Anna. — Juditha.

Martha. — Catarina.

𝔏angley.

ARMS. *Ermine, on a bend vert three leopards' faces or.*
CREST. *A cockatrice sable, combed and wattled gules.*

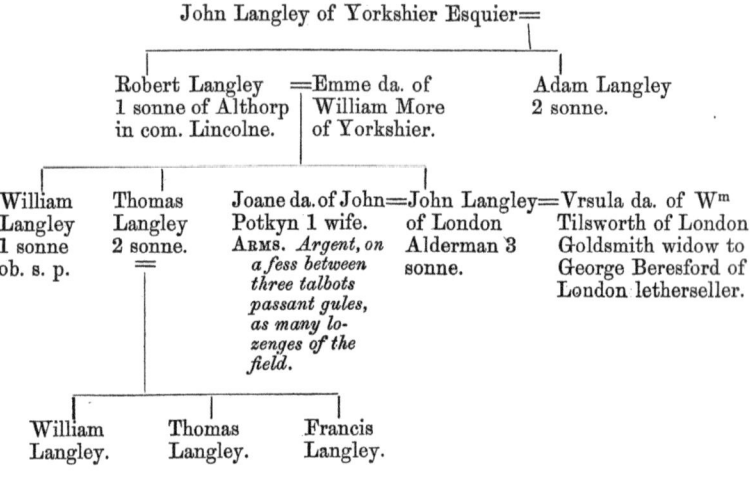

John Langley of Yorkshier Esquier=

Robert Langley =Emme da. of
1 sonne of Althorp | William More
in com. Lincolne. | of Yorkshier.

Adam Langley
2 sonne.

William Langley 1 sonne ob. s. p.

Thomas Langley 2 sonne. =

Joane da. of John Potkyn 1 wife. ARMS. *Argent, on a fess between three talbots passant gules, as many lozenges of the field.*=John Langley of London Alderman 3 sonne.=Vrsula da. of Wm Tilsworth of London Goldsmith widow to George Beresford of London letherseller.

William Langley.

Thomas Langley.

Francis Langley.

𝔄llen.

ARMS. *Per fesse sable and or, a pale engrailed counterchanged, on the first three talbots passant or, collared gules.*
CREST. *A talbot passant sable, collared gules, ears and chain or.*

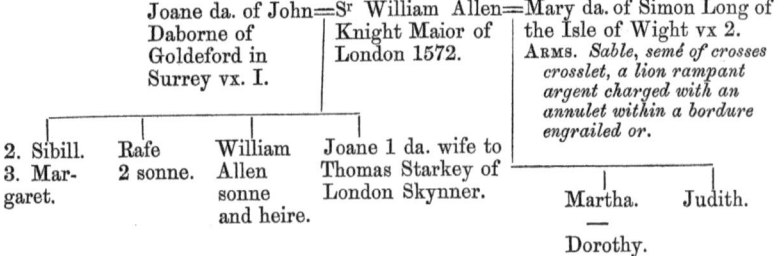

Joane da. of John Daborne of Goldeford in Surrey vx. I.=Sr William Allen Knight Maior of London 1572.=Mary da. of Simon Long of the Isle of Wight vx 2. ARMS. *Sable, semé of crosses crosslet, a lion rampant argent charged with an annulet within a bordure engrailed or.*

2. Sibill.
3. Margaret.

Rafe 2 sonne.

William Allen sonne and heire.

Joane 1 da. wife to Thomas Starkey of London Skynner.

Martha. Judith.

Dorothy.

Duckett.

ARMS. *Quarterly :*—1. *Sable, on a saltire argent a mullet for difference.* (DUCKETT.)
2. *Gules, three cushions ermine tasseled or.* (REDMAN.)   3. *Gules, a lion rampant argent, charged with a fleur-de-lis sable, within a bordure engrailed of the
second.* (ALDBOROUGH.)   4. *Gules, semée of crosses crosslet or, a saltire argent;
over all a mullet sable for difference.* (WINDESORE.)
CREST. *A lavender sheaf proper, banded or.*

Mary da. of Hugh Leighton=Sʳ Lionell Duckett=Jane da. of Humfrey Pakington
of Leighton in com. Salop. | Knight Maior of | Esq. vx. 2.
 | London. | *Arms, Quarterly :*—
 | | 1 and 4. *Per chevron sable and*
 | | *argent, in chief three mullets or,*
 | | *in base as many garbs gules.*
George Duckett | Thomas Duckett | 2. *Argent, on a fess between six*
died young. | sonne and heyre. | *martlets gules three quatrefoils.*
 | | (WASHBOURNE.)
 | | 3. *Argent, on a bend azure three*
 | | *martlets or.* (HARDING.)

Hawes.

ARMS. *Azure, on a chevron or three cinquefoils pierced purpure, a canton ermine.*
CREST. *Out of a ducal coronet or, a stag's-head argent attired of the first.*

Sʳ James Hawes Knight=Audrey da. of John Copwood.
Maior of London. | ARMS. *Argent, a pile in bend sable fimbriated
 | and engrailed gules between two eagles dis-
 | played vert.*

John | Margaret wife to | Elizabeth wife | Mary wife to John
Hawes | John Wattes of | to Thomas | Smith of London,
sonne | London, Clothworker. | Wilford. | Mercer.
& heire.

Rivers.

ARMS. *Azure, a fess engrailed argent, surmounted of another gules, charged with three
roses of the second.*
CREST. *Out of a bunch of reeds vert, a demi swan with wings expanded argent,
ducally gorged or.*

Sʳ John Rivers Knight Mayor of=Elizabeth da. of Sʳ George Barne of
London (in 1573). | London Knight.
 | *Arms, Quarterly :*—
 | 1 and 4. *Argent, on a chevron engrailed azure
 | three trefoils or, between as many Cornish
 | choughs sable.*
 | 2 and 3. *Argent, on a fess engrailed sable a rose
 | between two fleurs-de-lis argent between three
 | greyhounds' heads erased sable collared or.*

John Rivers | 3 Henry. | 5 William. | George Rivers | Edward | 1 Alice.
2 sonne. | 4 Richard. | | eldest. sonne | 6 sonne. | 2 Elizabeth.
 | | | | | 3 Dorothy.

Warren.

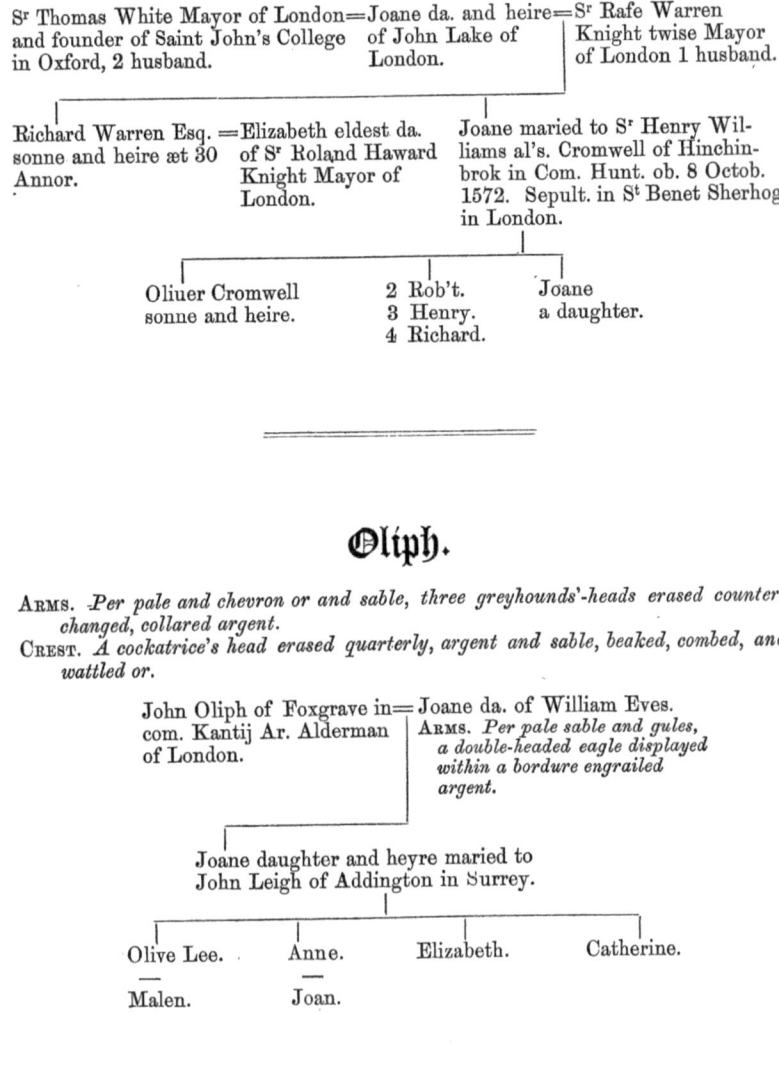

Sʳ Thomas White Mayor of London=Joane da. and heire=Sʳ Rafe Warren
and founder of Saint John's College   of John Lake of　　Knight twise Mayor
in Oxford, 2 husband.　　　　　　　London.　　　　　　of London 1 husband.

Richard Warren Esq. =Elizabeth eldest da.　Joane maried to Sʳ Henry Wil-
sonne and heire æt 30　of Sʳ Roland Haward　liams al's. Cromwell of Hinchin-
Annor.　　　　　　　Knight Mayor of　　brok in Com. Hunt. ob. 8 Octob.
　　　　　　　　　　London.　　　　　　1572. Sepult. in Sᵗ Benet Sherhog
　　　　　　　　　　　　　　　　　　in London.

Oliuer Cromwell　　2 Rob't.　Joane
sonne and heire.　　3 Henry.　a daughter.
　　　　　　　　　4 Richard.

Oliph.

ARMS. *Per pale and chevron or and sable, three greyhounds'-heads erased counter-*
　　changed, collared argent.
CREST. *A cockatrice's head erased quarterly, argent and sable, beaked, combed, and*
　　wattled or.

John Oliph of Foxgrave in= Joane da. of William Eves.
com. Kantij Ar. Alderman　ARMS. *Per pale sable and gules,*
of London.　　　　　　　*a double-headed eagle displayed*
　　　　　　　　　　　within a bordure engrailed
　　　　　　　　　　　argent.

Joane daughter and heyre maried to
John Leigh of Addington in Surrey.

Olive Lee.　　Anne.　　Elizabeth.　　Catherine.
　—　　　　　　—
Malen.　　　　Joan.

Beecher.

ARMS. *Vair gules and argent, on a canton or a stag's head caboshed sable.*
CREST. *A demi-lion erased argent, girded round the waist with a ducal coronet or.*

Henry Beecher of London Alderman=Alice d. of Thomas Heron
uxor ejus 2 da. Her coate was G on | of Croydon 1 wife.
a bend A betwene 6 martlets ar. a | ARMS. *Quarterly:*—1. *Gules, a chevron*
lions head erased gules, on the top | *engrailed between three herons statant*
of yᵉ bend, p' name Gittins. | *argent, beaked and legged or.* 2. *Ar-*
| *gent, two bends and in chief a cross*
| *crosslet sable.* 3. *Argent, a fess gules*
| *between three boars' heads couped sable.*
| 4. *Argent, a chevron engrailed gules*
| *between three bugle-horns sable.*

2. Edward   Henry   Elizabeth,   2. Mary.   3. Margaret.   4. Mabel.
   Beecher. Beecher   wife to Cle-
   —   sonne and ment Kelk
3. Vane   heyre.   of London.
   Beecher. —
4. William. 5. Bartholmew.

Bacon.

ARMS. *Quarterly:*—1 *and* 4. *Gules, on a chief argent two mullets sable.* 2 *and* 3.
Barry of six or and azure, a bend gules, over all a mullet for difference.
CREST. *A boar passant ermine, charged with a mullet for difference.*

John Bacon of Drinkeston in com. Suff. Esq.=
descended of Sʳ Edmond Bacon of Essex that
maried Margery da. and heyre of Quaplade.

Robert Bacon sonne=Isabell d. of John Cage of Perken-   John Bacon
and heyre.   ham in Suff.   2 sonne.

Thomas   Mary da. of   =James Bacon 3   =Margaret da. of Wᵐ Raw-   Sir Nichˢ
Bacon   John Gardner   sonne Alderman   lins of London Grocer   Bacon
1 sonne. of Grove   of London mar-   widow of Richard Gold-   Kᵗ 2 s.
         Place in com.   ried to his 3 wife ston of London salter.
         Buck. Esq.   Anne da. of   *Per pale sable and argent,*
                         Humphry Pak-   *on a fess between three*
                         ington widow of *martlets as many cres-*
                         Alderman Jack-   *cents, all counterchanged.*
                         man.

     Anne married to John   James Bacon   William Bacon
     Rivett of Bramston   1 sonne.   2 sonne.
     in com. Suff. gen.

C

Dane.

ARMS. *Or, a chevron engrailed azure between three hinds passant gules.*
CREST. *A wolf statant argent.*

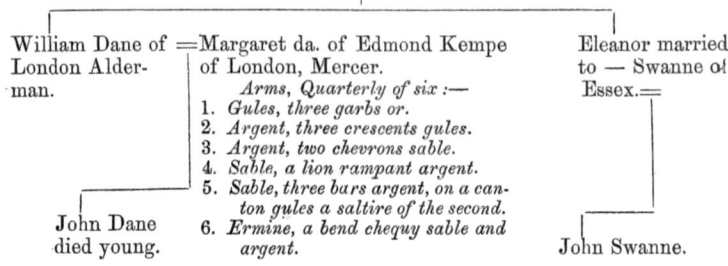

John Dane of Stortford in=Alice d. of — Peppercorne.
com. Hertf. gent.

William Dane of =Margaret da. of Edmond Kempe
London Alder-   of London, Mercer.
man.   *Arms, Quarterly of six :—*
                1. *Gules, three garbs or.*
                2. *Argent, three crescents gules.*
                3. *Argent, two chevrons sable.*
                4. *Sable, a lion rampant argent.*
John Dane   5. *Sable, three bars argent, on a can-*
died young.   *ton gules a saltire of the second.*
                6. *Ermine, a bend chequy sable and*
                   argent.

Eleanor married
to — Swanne of
Essex.=

John Swanne.

Boxe.

ARMS. *Azure, a lion passant argent, between three griffins' heads erased or.*

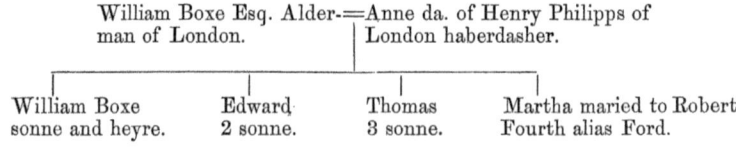

William Boxe Esq. Alder-=Anne da. of Henry Philipps of
man of London.   London haberdasher.

William Boxe   Edward   Thomas   Martha maried to Robert
sonne and heyre.   2 sonne.   3 sonne.   Fourth alias Ford.

Pipe.

ARMS. *Azure, a fess and two bars gemelles between six cross crosslets or.*
CREST. *A demi-pegasus, wings expanded argent.*

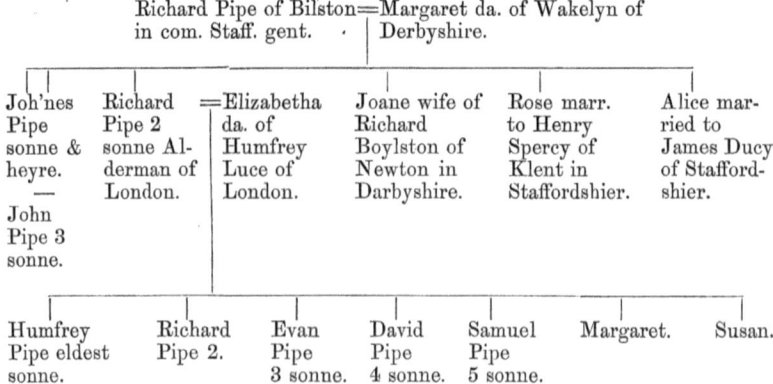

Richard Pipe of Bilston=Margaret da. of Wakelyn of
in com. Staff. gent. · Derbyshire.

Joh'nes   Richard   =Elizabetha   Joane wife of   Rose marr.   Alice mar-
Pipe   Pipe 2   da. of   Richard   to Henry   ried to
sonne &   sonne Al-   Humfrey   Boylston of   Spercy of   James Ducy
heyre.   derman of   Luce of   Newton in   Klent in   of Stafford-
—   London.   London.   Darbyshire.   Staffordshier. shier.
John
Pipe 3
sonne.

Humfrey   Richard   Evan   David   Samuel   Margaret.   Susan.
Pipe eldest Pipe 2.   Pipe   Pipe   Pipe
sonne.   3 sonne.   4 sonne.   5 sonne.

Mylles.

ARMS. *Quarterly*:—1 *and* 4. *Ermine, a millrind sable.* 2. *Per pale gules and azure, three lions rampant ermine.* 3. *Or, a saltire sable between four cherries within a bordure engrailed of the second.*
CREST. *A lion rampant or.*

Mylles of the Cyty of =— his wife d. of — Merry.
London A° D'ni 1568. ARMS. *Gules, on a fess engrailed between three water bougets erminois as many crosses pattées sable.*

Leigh.

ARMS. *Gules, a cross engrailed argent, in the dexter chief a lozenge.*
CREST. *A unicorn's head couped or.*

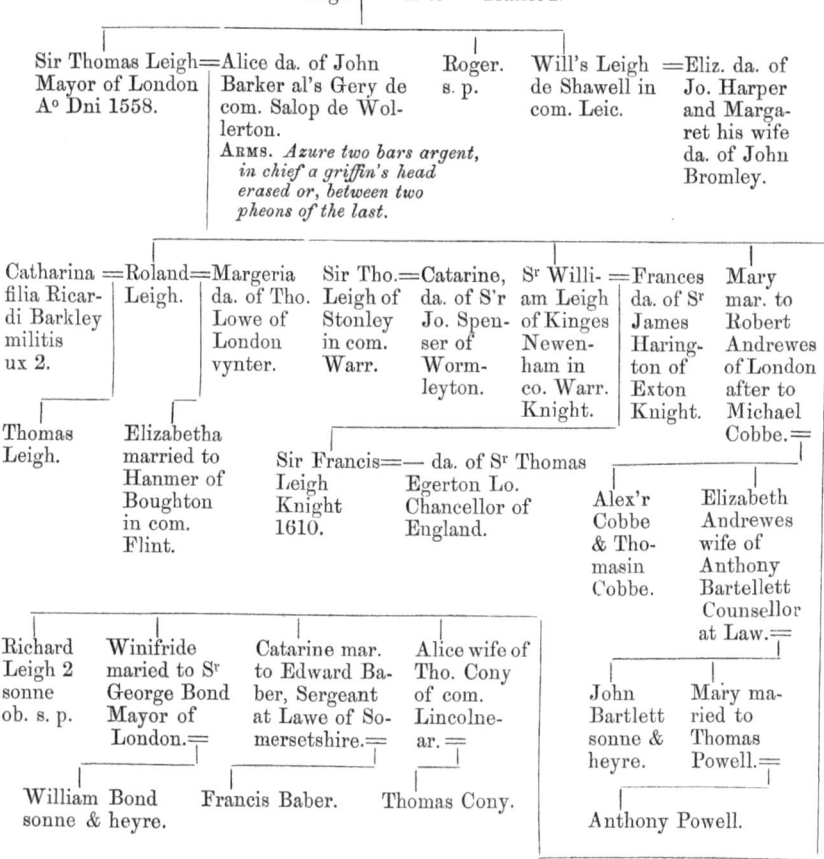

— Legh=— d. to — Trafford.

Sir Thomas Leigh=Alice da. of John | Roger. | Will's Leigh =Eliz. da. of
Mayor of London | Barker al's Gery de | s. p. | de Shawell in | Jo. Harper
A° Dni 1558. | com. Salop de Wol- | | com. Leic. | and Marga-
| lerton. | | | ret his wife
| ARMS. *Azure two bars argent,* | | | da. of John
| *in chief a griffin's head* | | | Bromley.
| *erased or, between two* | | |
| *pheons of the last.* | | |

Catharina =Roland=Margeria | Sir Tho.=Catarine, | Sr Willi- =Frances | Mary
filia Ricar- | Leigh. | da. of Tho. | Leigh of | da. of Sr | am Leigh | da. of Sr | mar. to
di Barkley | | Lowe of | Stonley | Jo. Spen- | of Kinges | James | Robert
militis | | London | in com. | ser of | Newen- | Haring- | Andrewes
ux 2. | | vynter. | Warr. | Worm- | ham in | ton of | of London
| | | | leyton. | co. Warr. | Exton | after to
| | | | | Knight. | Knight. | Michael
| | | | | | | Cobbe.=

Thomas | Elizabetha | Sir Francis=— da. of Sr Thomas | Alex'r | Elizabeth
Leigh. | married to | Leigh | Egerton Lo. | Cobbe | Andrewes
| Hanmer of | Knight | Chancellor of | & Tho- | wife of
| Boughton | 1610. | England. | masin | Anthony
| in com. | | | Cobbe. | Bartellett
| Flint. | | | | Counsellor
| | | | | at Law.=

Richard | Winifride | Catarine mar. | Alice wife of | John | Mary ma-
Leigh 2 | maried to Sr | to Edward Ba- | Tho. Cony | Bartlett | ried to
sonne | George Bond | ber, Sergeant | of com. | sonne & | Thomas
ob. s. p. | Mayor of | at Lawe of So- | Lincolne- | heyre. | Powell.=
| London.= | mersetshire.= | ar. |

William Bond | Francis Baber. | Thomas Cony. | Anthony Powell.
sonne & heyre.

𝔚odroff.

ARMS. *Quarterly :—1 and 4. Gules, on a chevron (argent) three bucks' heads erased (sable), a chief per fess nebulée (sable and argent). 2 and 3. Sable, a fess ermine between two lions passant guardant argent.*

CREST. *A dexter arm embowed, habited with leaves vert, holding in the hand a branch of honeysuckle, all proper.*

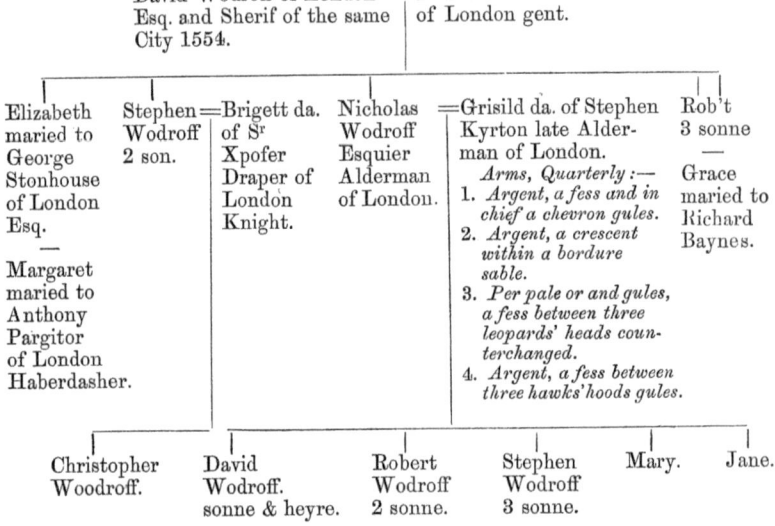

David Wodroff of London Esq. and Sherif of the same City 1554. =Elizabeth da. of John Hill of London gent.

Elizabeth maried to George Stonhouse of London Esq. —
Margaret maried to Anthony Pargitor of London Haberdasher.

Stephen Wodroff 2 son. =Brigett da. of Sr Xpofer Draper of London Knight.

Nicholas Wodroff Esquier Alderman of London. =Grisild da. of Stephen Kyrton late Alderman of London.
Arms, Quarterly :—
1. *Argent, a fess and in chief a chevron gules.*
2. *Argent, a crescent within a bordure sable.*
3. *Per pale or and gules, a fess between three leopards' heads counterchanged.*
4. *Argent, a fess between three hawks' hoods gules.*

Rob't 3 sonne —
Grace maried to Richard Baynes.

Christopher Woodroff.

David Wodroff. sonne & heyre.

Robert Wodroff 2 sonne.

Stephen Wodroff 3 sonne.

Mary.

Jane.

Blanck.

ARMS. *Per fess sable and ermine a pale counterchanged, on the first three demi-lions rampant or.*

CREST. *A dragon's head couped vert, collared and chained argent, holding in the mouth a firebrand of the last flamed proper.*

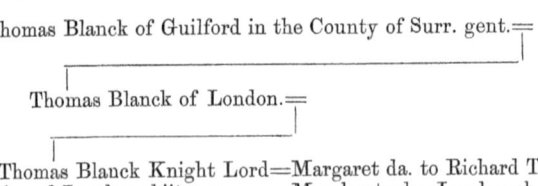

Thomas Blanck of Guilford in the County of Surr. gent.=

Thomas Blanck of London.=

Sr Thomas Blanck Knight Lord Maior of London obijt s. p. =Margaret da. to Richard Traves Marchantaylor London ob. s. p.
ARMS. *Argent, a saltire between four butterflies volant sable.*

Harvy.

ARMS. *Or, on a chevron between three leopards' heads gules a crescent of the field.*
CREST. *A leopard passant argent spotted sable, ducally gorged and chained or, reflexed over back.*

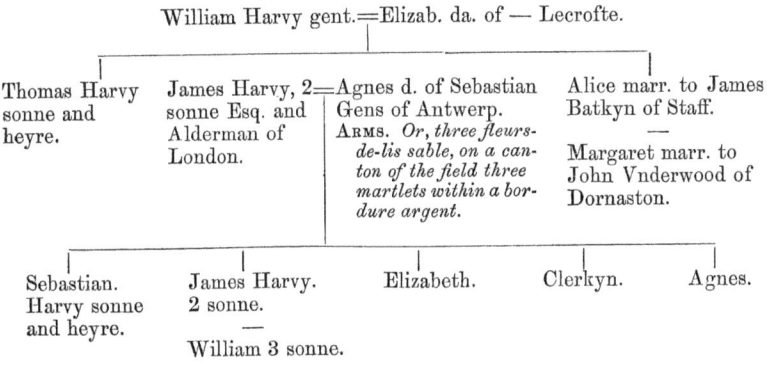

William Harvy gent.=Elizab. da. of — Lecrofte.

Thomas Harvy sonne and heyre.	James Harvy, 2 sonne Esq. and Alderman of London.	=Agnes d. of Sebastian Gens of Antwerp. ARMS. *Or, three fleurs-de-lis sable, on a canton of the field three martlets within a bordure argent.*	Alice marr. to James Batkyn of Staff. — Margaret marr. to John Vnderwood of Dornaston.

Sebastian. Harvy sonne and heyre.

James Harvy. 2 sonne. — William 3 sonne.

Elizabeth.

Clerkyn.

Agnes.

Branche.

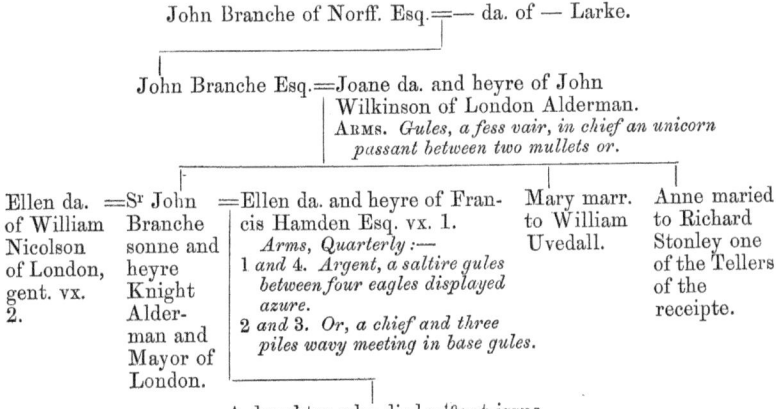

ARMS. *Quarterly:*—1 *and* 4. *Argent, a lion rampant gules, debruised by a bendlet sable.* 2 *and* 3. *Gules, a fess vair, in chief an unicorn passant between two mullets or.* (WILKINSON.)
CREST. *Out of a ducal coronet or a cockatrice's head azure beaked or, combed and wattled gules.*

John Branche of Norff. Esq.=— da. of — Larke.

John Branche Esq.=Joane da. and heyre of John Wilkinson of London Alderman.
ARMS. *Gules, a fess vair, in chief an unicorn passant between two mullets or.*

Ellen da. of William Nicolson of London, gent. vx. 2.

=Sr John Branche sonne and heyre Knight Alderman and Mayor of London.

=Ellen da. and heyre of Francis Hamden Esq. vx. 1.
Arms, Quarterly:—
1 *and* 4. *Argent, a saltire gules between four eagles displayed azure.*
2 *and* 3. *Or, a chief and three piles wavy meeting in base gules.*

Mary marr. to William Uvedall.

Anne married to Richard Stonley one of the Tellers of the receipte.

A daughter who died w^th^out issue.

Gamage.

ARMS. *Quarterly :*—1 *and* 4. *Argent, a bend lozengy gules, on a chief azure three escallops or.* 2 *and* 3. *Gules fretty vair.* (HORNE.)

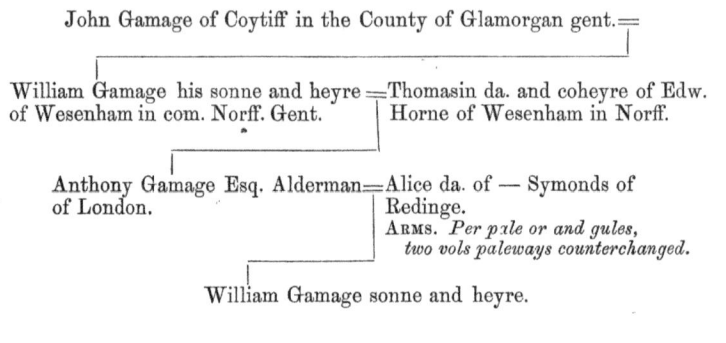

John Gamage of Coytiff in the County of Glamorgan gent.=

William Gamage his sonne and heyre =Thomasin da. and coheyre of Edw.
of Wesenham in com. Norff. Gent. | Horne of Wesenham in Norff.

Anthony Gamage Esq. Alderman=Alice da. of — Symonds of
of London. | Redinge.
| ARMS. *Per pale or and gules,*
| *two vols paleways counterchanged.*

William Gamage sonne and heyre.

Sebright.

ARMS. *Quarterly :*—1 *and* 4. *Argent, three cinquefoils sable.* 2. *Azure, six bezants, three, two, and one.* (BYSETT.) 3. *Or, a saltire gules surmounted by a fess sable.* (ASHE.)
CREST. *An heraldic tiger sejant argent, tufted and ducally crowned or.*

Edward Sebright of Blakeshall in the County of Worceter gent as apeareth most manifestly vpon the deliberate view and p'vsing of sundry very fayre and auntient deedes, charters and records of great creditt and authority is lineally descended of the body of Peter Sebright of Sebrights hall in the County of Essex Esq. wch Peter also descended of the body of Sr Walter Sebright of Sebrightes hall Knight who lyued in the tyme of the reigne of King Henry the second, W^ch name and family of the Sebrightes as evidently apeareth by most auncient recordes beareth *Silver 3 Cinquefoyles sable pierced of the field,* And also as most evidently apeareth by a most fayre and auncient deede bearing date at Sebrightes hall the Tewesday next after the feast of St John Baptist in the 22 yeare of the raigne of King Edward the first the sayd Sr Walter did lineally descend of the body of One of the heyres generall of Manserus Bysett a Baron sewer to King Henry the first, wch Manserus Bisett I do fynde as well by the auncient recordes of my Office as by the sight of an ould deede, made by the said Manserus and sealed with his Seale of Armes did beare *Azure 6 besantes gould,* And I do also fynde by view of another auncient deede that in the reigne of King Henry the second William Sebright of Sebrightes hall married Elizabeth the daughter and sole heyre of Sir Henry de Ashe Knight wch Sr Henry I do also fynde by the said auncient recordes did beare, *Gould a saltier goules a fess Sables.*

Osborne.

ARMS. *Quarterly :—1 and 4. Quarterly ermine and azure, a cross or. 2. Argent, two bars gules, on a quarter of the second a cross of the first ; in chief a crescent of the last for difference. 3. Argent, a chevron vert between three annulets gules.*
CREST. *An heraldic tiger passant or, tufted and maned sable, charged with an ogress.*

Sr Edward Osborne Knight Cloth-worker & Mayor of London. =— his wife daughter of — Hewett.
ARMS. *Azure, on a fess flory counterflory between three lions passant argent as many lapwings proper.*

Gresham.

ARMS. *Argent, a chevron ermine between three mullets pierced sable.*
CREST. *On a mound a grasshopper vert.*

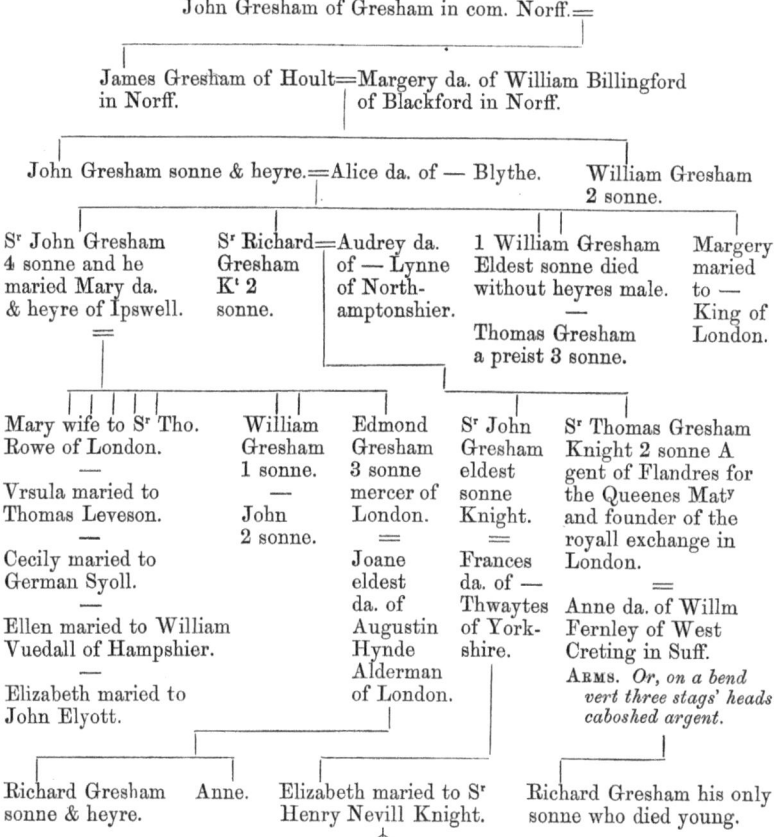

John Gresham of Gresham in com. Norff.=

James Gresham of Hoult=Margery da. of William Billingford in Norff. | of Blackford in Norff.

John Gresham sonne & heyre.=Alice da. of — Blythe. | William Gresham 2 sonne.

Sr John Gresham 4 sonne and he maried Mary da. & heyre of Ipswell. =

Sr Richard=Audrey da. Gresham of — Lynne Kt 2 of North-sonne. amptonshier.

1 William Gresham Eldest sonne died without heyres male.
—
Thomas Gresham a preist 3 sonne.

Margery maried to — King of London.

Mary wife to Sr Tho. Rowe of London.
—
Vrsula maried to Thomas Leveson.
—
Cecily maried to German Syoll.
—
Ellen maried to William Vuedall of Hampshier.
—
Elizabeth maried to John Elyott.

William Gresham 1 sonne.
—
John 2 sonne.

Edmond Gresham 3 sonne mercer of London. = Joane eldest da. of Augustin Hynde Alderman of London.

Sr John Gresham eldest sonne Knight. = Frances da. of — Thwaytes of York-shire.

Sr Thomas Gresham Knight 2 sonne A gent of Flandres for the Queenes Maty and founder of the royall exchange in London. = Anne da. of Willm Fernley of West Creting in Suff.
ARMS. *Or, on a bend vert three stags' heads caboshed argent.*

Richard Gresham sonne & heyre. Anne.

Elizabeth maried to Sr Henry Nevill Knight.

Richard Gresham his only sonne who died young.

Dyxye.

ARMS. *Quarterly:—1 and 4. Azure, a lion rampant and a chief or. 2 and 3. Argent,
a saltire engrailed between four escallops sable.*
CREST. *A lynx sejant argent, ducally gorged or.*

Sr Wolston Dyxye=Anna daughter of Sr Xpofer Draper of London,
Knight Maior of Knight and Mayor.
London died *Arms, Quarterly:—*
wthout issue 1. *Argent, on a fess between three annulets gules a mullet*
A^o D^m 1593.   *argent between two covered cups or.* (DRAPER.)
      2. *Argent, on two chevrons between three escallops sable*
       six martlets or. (DRAPER.)
      3. *Ermine, on a chief azure three lions rampant or.*
       (AUCHER.)
      4. *Ermine, a fess chequy sable and argent.* (ERSWICK.)

Cosworth.

ARMS. *Argent, on a chevron between three falcons' wings azure five bezants.*
CREST. *A wyvern's head couped azure, purfled or, langued gules.*

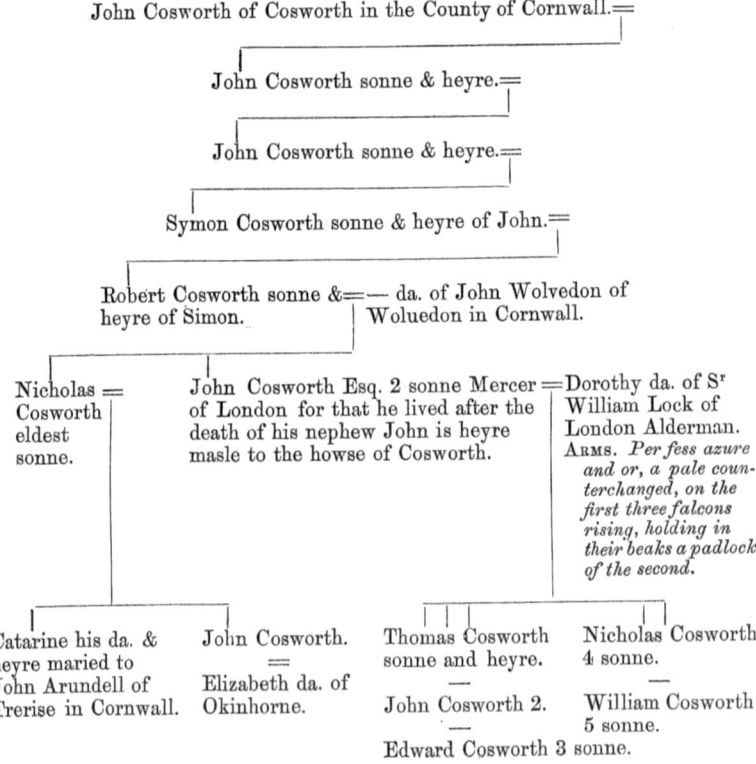

John Cosworth of Cosworth in the County of Cornwall.=

John Cosworth sonne & heyre.=

John Cosworth sonne & heyre.=

Symon Cosworth sonne & heyre of John.=

Robert Cosworth sonne &=— da. of John Wolvedon of
heyre of Simon. | Woluedon in Cornwall.

Nicholas = John Cosworth Esq. 2 sonne Mercer =Dorothy da. of S^r
Cosworth of London for that he lived after the William Lock of
eldest   death of his nephew John is heyre London Alderman.
sonne.   masle to the howse of Cosworth. ARMS. *Per fess azure
            and or, a pale coun-
            terchanged, on the
            first three falcons
            rising, holding in
            their beaks a padlock
            of the second.*

Catarine his da. & John Cosworth. Thomas Cosworth Nicholas Cosworth
heyre maried to =   sonne and heyre. 4 sonne.
John Arundell of Elizabeth da. of —
Trerise in Cornwall. Okinhorne. John Cosworth 2. William Cosworth
          —   5 sonne.
         Edward Cosworth 3 sonne.

Egerton.

ARMS. *Quarterly :—*1. *Sable, a chevron between three pheons argent.* 2. *Ermine, a fess gules, fretty or.* 3. *Argent, a chevron between three water-bougets sable.* 4. *Vert, a chevron between three talbots passant argent.*
CREST. *A stag's head erased or.*

William Egerton Esq. descended of a younger══ — daughter of — Welbeck
howse of Egerton of Wrinehill in Cheshier. │ of London.

William Egerton
1 sonne.

Thomas Egerton══Anne da. of — Langton of Hartfordshire
Mercer of │ who was of the howse of Langton of
London. │ Yorkshier.
│ ARMS. *Argent, three chevrons gules.*

| Timothy Egerton eldest sonne. | Lionell Egerton 2 sonne. | Thomas Egerton 3 sonne. | Randall. 4. Stephen. 5. Arthur. 6. | Mary 1 da. maried to John Wedgwood. | Anne 2 daughter. |

Isham.

ARMS. *Gules, three piles wavy meeting in base or, over all a fess of the second.*
ANOTHER. *Gules, three piles wavy, meeting in the fess point, and a fess wavy argent.*
CREST. *A demi-swan wings endorsed argent, gutté de larmes.*

William Isham of Pitesley══Ellen da. of — Vere of
descended as heyre male of │ Adington in com.
the howse of Isham in │ p'dict Esq.
com. Northampton.

Ewseby Isham sonne and heyre══Anne da. of Giles Powlton of
of William. │ Desborow in com. Northt. gent.

Giles Isham══
1 sonne.

Anne.
—
Jane.
—
Margery.

Robert
a clerk
2 sonne

Gregory 3 sonne
late of London
Marchaunt and
since of Bram-
stone in the
county of
Northampton.

John Isham 4══Eliz. da.
sonne of Lam- │ of Ni-
portal's.Lang- │ cholas
port in com. │ Barker
Northampton │ of Lon-
Esq. and also │ don.
Mercer of
London.

Henry
5 sonne
controller
for the
Custome
inwards
to
Queene
Eliz.

Ewseby Isham
only sonne and
heyre.

Thomas Isham 1 sonne.
—
Henry 2.
—
Richard 3.
—
Robert 4.

Anne 1 da.

Elizabeth 2

𝔚𝔞𝔩𝔨𝔢𝔡𝔢𝔫.

ARMS. *Argent, a chevron engrailed between three griffins' heads erased azure, on a chief of the last an anchor or between two bezants.*
CREST. *A griffin's head erased quarterly argent and vert, beaked, ducally gorged, and ears or.*

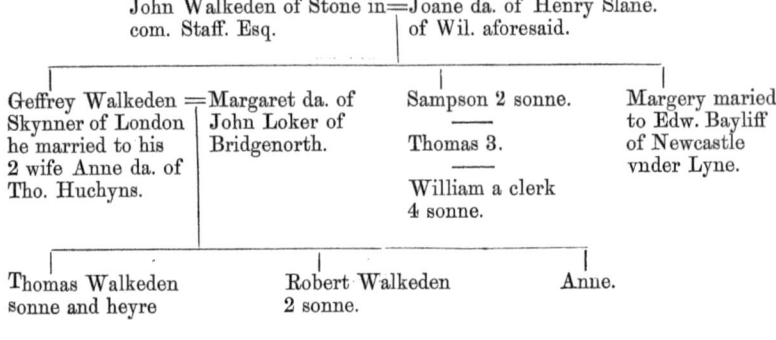

John Walkeden of Stone in=Joane da. of Henry Slane.
com. Staff. Esq. | of Wil. aforesaid.

Geffrey Walkeden =Margaret da. of
Skynner of London | John Loker of
he married to his | Bridgenorth.
2 wife Anne da. of
Tho. Huchyns.

Sampson 2 sonne.
——
Thomas 3.
——
William a clerk
4 sonne.

Margery maried
to Edw. Bayliff
of Newcastle
vnder Lyne.

Thomas Walkeden
sonne and heyre

Robert Walkeden
2 sonne.

Anne.

ℌ𝔞𝔯𝔡𝔦𝔫𝔤.

[ARMS. *Argent, on a bend azure three martlets or, on a sinister canton of the second a rose or, between two fleurs-de-lis of the field.*
CREST. *A demi-antelope proper, horned or, holding in his paws an anchor reversed.*]

=Robert Harding Alderman & Sheriff of London had 2 wifes.=

𝔏𝔢𝔳𝔢𝔰𝔬𝔫.

ARMS. *Quarterly:—1 and 4. Azure, a fess nebulé argent and sable, between three leaves or. 2 and 3. Argent, a chevron gules between three cinquefoils pierced sable.*
CREST. *A goat's head erased argent, attired or.*

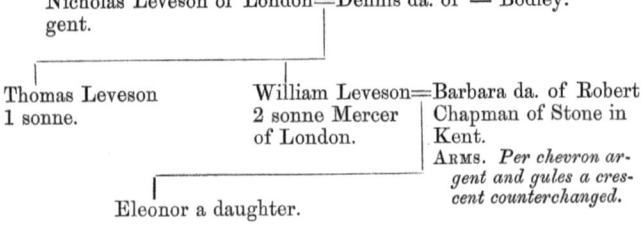

Nicholas Leveson of London=Dennis da. of — Bodley.
gent.

Thomas Leveson
1 sonne.

William Leveson=Barbara da. of Robert
2 sonne Mercer | Chapman of Stone in
of London. | Kent.
| ARMS. *Per chevron ar-*
| *gent and gules a cres-*
| *cent counterchanged.*

Eleonor a daughter.

Lowen.

ARMS. *Quarterly :—1 and 4. Quarterly per fess embattled or and azure, three stags' heads caboshed counterchanged. 2 and 3. Per chevron flory counterflory argent and gules, three martlets counterchanged.*

CREST. *A stag statant quarterly, per pale indented or and azure, the sinister horn of the first, the dexter of the last.*

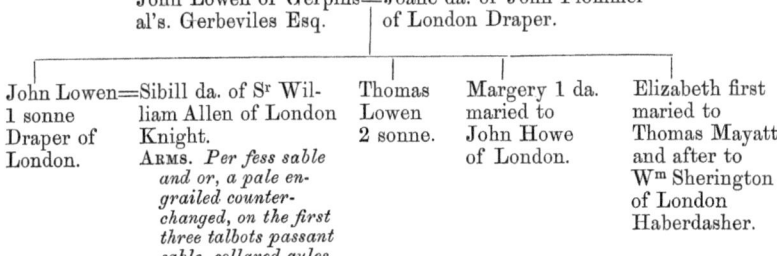

John Lowen of Gerpins=Joane da. of John Plommer
al's. Gerbeviles Esq. | of London Draper.

John Lowen=Sibill da. of Sr William Allen of London
1 sonne | Knight.
Draper of | ARMS. *Per fess sable*
London. | *and or, a pale en-*
| *grailed counter-*
| *changed, on the first*
| *three talbots passant*
| *sable, collared gules.*

Thomas Lowen 2 sonne.

Margery 1 da. maried to John Howe of London.

Elizabeth first maried to Thomas Mayatt and after to Wm Sherington of London Haberdasher.

Rivett.

ARMS. *Quarterly :—1 and 4. Argent, three bars sable, in chief as many trivets of the last. 2 and 3. Per pale argent and sable, on a chevron between three lozenges, as many martlets, all counterchanged.*

CREST. *An arm erect, couped at the elbow, per pale argent and sable, cuffed per pale of the second and first, holding in the hand proper a sword broken of the first, the handle of the second, hilt and pommel or.*

Thomas Rivett of Stow Markett=Joane da. — Raven of Needom
in Suff. Esq. | in Suff.

James Rivett 1 sonne
ARMS. 1 *and* 4. *Sable on a cross engrailed between four eagles displayed argent, five lions passant of the field.* 2 *and* 3. *Two bars and on a canton gules a cinquefoil or.*

Grisild da. of Willm Lord Pagett.

=Thomas Rivett 2 sonne of Chippenham Cambrigeshier, also Citizen & Mercer of London who fined for his shrivalty 1566.

=Alice eldest da. of Sr John Cotton of Landwade in Cambridgeshier his 1 wife.

John Rivett 3 sonne.
—
William Rivett 4 sonne.

Mirabell maried to Wm Birde of London.

Mirabell 1 da.

Alice 2 da.

Browne.

ARMS. *Quarterly :—*1 *and* 4. *Argent, a chevron between three cranes sable.* 2 *and* 3.
Sable, semé of crosses pattée fitchée, a lion rampant or.
CREST. *An heraldic tiger azure, tufted or.*

John Browne of Bekonsfeilde═— daughter of John Stoke
in com. Buck.   of Carleton in com. Bedf.

John Browne sonne and═— da. of Nicholas Bally
heyre.   of Romford in Essex.

Robert Browne sonne and═— da. of William Gardiner.
heyre of John

John Browne, gent.═Alice da. and one of the heyres of
       Henry Tillesworth.

Robert Browne ═Margaret da. of John	Thomas ═Alice da. of	Elizabeth
of London Lucas of Halden and	Browne Thomas	maried to
sonne and heyre cosin and heyre of	2 sonne. Chapman	Thomas
of John — Lucas.	al's Chapell.	Tedwaye.

Arms, Quarterly :—
1. *Argent, a fess between six annulets sable.*
2. *Azure, a fess between three stags statant argent.* (HILLES.)
3. *Argent, two talbots courant gules.* (PENNE.)
4. *Sable, fretty or, a martlet for difference.* (BRACKENBY.)
5. *Sable, a chevron or between three daggers erect argent.* (BAILNALL.)
6. *Gules, two bars and an orle of martlets or.* (PAINELL.)

Dorothy maried	Jane mar.	William═Anne da. of	Thomas
to Robert	to Willm	Browne Thurstan	Browne 2.
Trappes of	Salkyns	sonne Collier of	—
London gent.	of London,	and Staffordshier.	Mary.
	gent.	heyre.	—
			Hester.

Thurstan Browne.   Margaret.   Mirabell.

Smyth.

ARMS. *Or, on a chief sable a lion passant of the first.*
CREST. *An heraldic tiger ermine, maned and tufted or.*

Randolf Smyth of Ratsdale=Margaret da. of Hamer.
in com. Lancastriæ.

Richard Smyth Citizen and=Margaret da. of Anthony Creede
Fishmonger of London. of Wiltshier.

Thomas Smyth sonne and heyre.

Trappes.

ARMS. *Quarterly:—1 and 4. Argent, three caltraps sable. 2 and 3. Azure, a
chevron between three crosses pattée or.*
CREST. *A man's head couped at the shoulders, attired gules, garnished or, on the head
a steel helmet, all proper, surmounted by a plume of three feathers argent.*

1st wife=Robert Trappes Citizen and=Joane da. of
Gouldsmith of London. — Crippes.

| Philip maried to Sr George Gifford Knt. | Robert Trappes Citizen and Mercer of London. | =Dorothy da. of Robt. Browne of London, gent. *Arms, Quarterly of eight:—* 1. *Argent, a chevron between three cranes sable.* (BROWNE.) 2. *Sable, semé of crosses pattée fitchée, a lion rampant or.* (TILLESWORTH.) 3. (LUCAS.) 4. (HILLES.) 5. (PENNE.) 6. (BRACKENBY.) 7. (BAILNAL.) 8. (PAINELL.) See Browne pedigree, p. 20. | Francis Trappes 2 sonne duxit Franciscam filiam Bawde de com. Linc. (ux 1) 2d duxit Annam filiam Burnham de Knaresborough. | Joyce first maried to — Saxy after to — Frankelyn. |

| Robert Trappes 1 sonne. Robert sine prole. | 2 Rowland maried Fr. Haile d. of Will. Haile died sans issue Sheriff of Surry 1616. | 3 Roger. Roger. | 4 Rafe. — 5 Giles. — 6 Andrew. | Dorothy wife of Pie, and 2 of Atkinson of Ouborn. | Joane 1 daughter by his first wife. Frances 2 daughter by his first wife. Mary 3 da. by his 2 wife. |

Salkyns.

ARMS. *Quarterly :—1 and 4. Or, two bars between three martlets sable. 2 and 3. Gules, a chevron argent, between three trefoils slipped ermine.*
CREST. *A lynx, sable.*

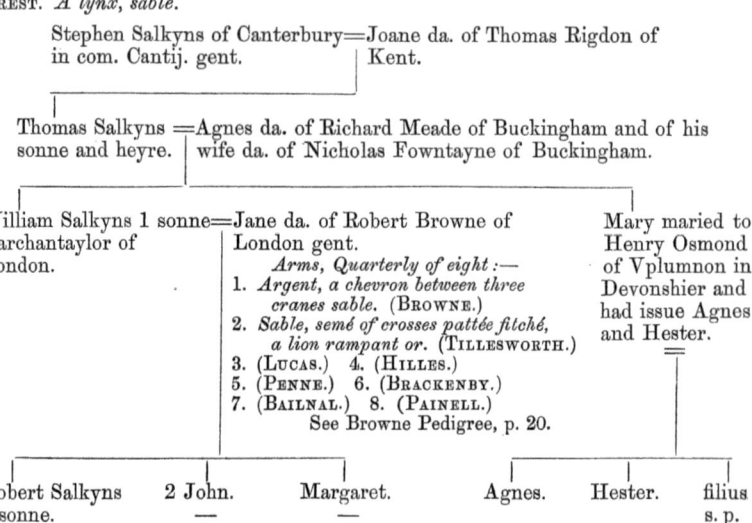

Stephen Salkyns of Canterbury=Joane da. of Thomas Rigdon of
in com. Cantij. gent. | Kent.

Thomas Salkyns =Agnes da. of Richard Meade of Buckingham and of his
sonne and heyre. | wife da. of Nicholas Fowntayne of Buckingham.

William Salkyns 1 sonne=Jane da. of Robert Browne of   Mary maried to
marchantaylor of   London gent.   Henry Osmond
London.   *Arms, Quarterly of eight :—*   of Vplumnon in
                 1. *Argent, a chevron between three*   Devonshier and
                    cranes sable. (BROWNE.)   had issue Agnes
                 2. *Sable, semé of crosses pattée fitché,*   and Hester.
                    a lion rampant or. (TILLESWORTH.)
                 3. (LUCAS.)   4. (HILLES.)
                 5. (PENNE.)   6. (BRACKENBY.)
                 7. (BAILNAL.)   8. (PAINELL.)
                    See Browne Pedigree, p. 20.

Robert Salkyns   2 John.   Margaret.   Agnes.   Hester.   filius
1 sonne.   s. p.
                3 Thomas.   Vrsula.

Dod.

ARMS. *Argent, on a fess gules between two cotises wavy sable three crescents or.*
CREST. *A serpent azure, issuing from and piercing a garb argent.*

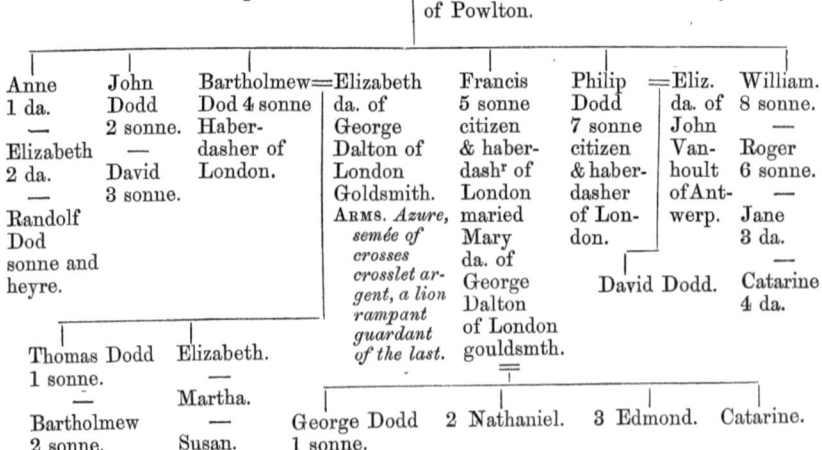

David Dod of Edge in com. Cestr.=Catarine da. of Nicholas Manley
                                   of Powlton.

Anne   John   Bartholmew=Elizabeth   Francis   Philip =Eliz.   William.
1 da.   Dodd   Dod 4 sonne   da. of   5 sonne   Dodd   da. of   8 sonne.
—   2 sonne.   Haber-   George   citizen   7 sonne   John   —
Elizabeth   —   dasher of   Dalton of   & haber-   citizen   Van-   Roger
2 da.   David   London.   London   dashᵣ of   & haber-   hoult   6 sonne.
—   3 sonne.   Goldsmith.   London   dasher   ofAnt-   —
Randolf   ARMS. *Azure,*   maried   of Lon-   werp.   Jane
Dod   *semée of*   Mary   don.   3 da.
sonne and   *crosses*   da. of   —
heyre.   *crosslet ar-*   George   David Dodd.   Catarine
                      gent, a lion   Dalton   4 da.
                      rampant   of London
                      guardant   gouldsmth.
Thomas Dodd   Elizabeth.   *of the last.*
1 sonne.   —
-          Martha.
Bartholmew   —   George Dodd   2 Nathaniel.   3 Edmond.   Catarine.
2 sonne.   Susan.   1 sonne.

𝔉airfax.

ARMS. *Argent, a lion rampant sable, surmounted by three bars gemelles gules.*
CREST. *A lion's head erased sable, charged with three bars gemelles and a mullet in chief or.*

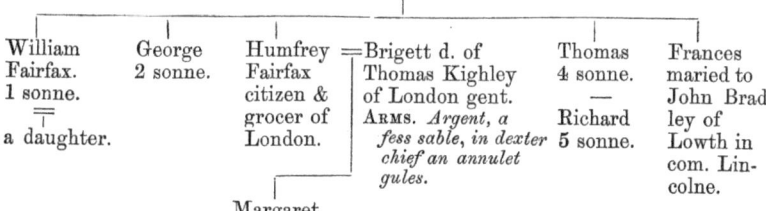

John Fairrefax of Lincolnshier=Anne da. of — Wooddis of
descended of a younger howse | Sussex.
in Yorkshier.

William Fairfax. 1 sonne. ᵀ a daughter.	George 2 sonne.	Humfrey =Brigett d. of Fairfax	Thomas 4 sonne.	Frances maried to

William
Fairfax.
1 sonne.
═
a daughter.

George
2 sonne.

Humfrey =Brigett d. of
Fairfax | Thomas Kighley
citizen & | of London gent.
grocer of | ARMS. *Argent, a*
London. | *fess sable, in dexter*
 | *chief an annulet*
 | *gules.*
 |
 Margaret.

Thomas
4 sonne.
—
Richard
5 sonne.

Frances
maried to
John Brad-
ley of
Lowth in
com. Lin-
colne.

𝔏e 𝔗aylor.

ARMS. *Quarterly :—1 and 4. Sable, a lion passant argent. 2. Or, a lion rampant guardant gules, collared argent. 3. Argent, a chevron gules between three eagles displayed sable.*
CREST. *A lynx proper.*

Thomas le Taylor de Carleill in=Jane da. of — Egleonby Esq.
com. Cumb'land.

John le Taylor of Carleill Esq.=Isabell da. of — Townes of Northumberland.

Thomas le Taylor of Lidgate in=Mary da. and heyre of John
com. Suff. ar. | Beniclere Esq.

Thomas le Taylor of Lidgate in Suff. Esq.=Elizab. da. and heyre of Richard Sely.

John le Taylor of Lidgate and of=Elizabeth da. of John Helder
Stechworth in com. Suff. Ar. | of Suff.

Thomas le Taylor, 1 sonne slayne at Mottrell s. p.	Edmond Taylor, 2 sonne slayne at Muscleboroughe feilde s. p.	John le =Bethsabe da. of Taylor 3	Edward Hall sonne of	of London Esq. London,	Esq.	Isaac Taylor 4 sonne.	Joane maried to Richard Hildersham.

Thomas le
Taylor,
1 sonne
slayne at
Mottrell
s. p.

Edmond
Taylor,
2 sonne
slayne at
Muscle-
boroughe
feilde s. p.

John le =Bethsabe da. of
Taylor 3 | Edward Hall
sonne of | of London Esq.
London, |
Esq. |
 Elizabetha
 vnica filia.

Isaac
Taylor
4 sonne.

Joane maried
to Richard
Hildersham.
———
Margaret
maried to
William Cock.

Browne.

ARMS. *Azure, on a chevron between three escallops or, within a bordure engrailed gules a crescent of the last.*

CREST. *A crane statant azure, beaked gules, winged and collared or, charged on the breast with a crescent of the last.*

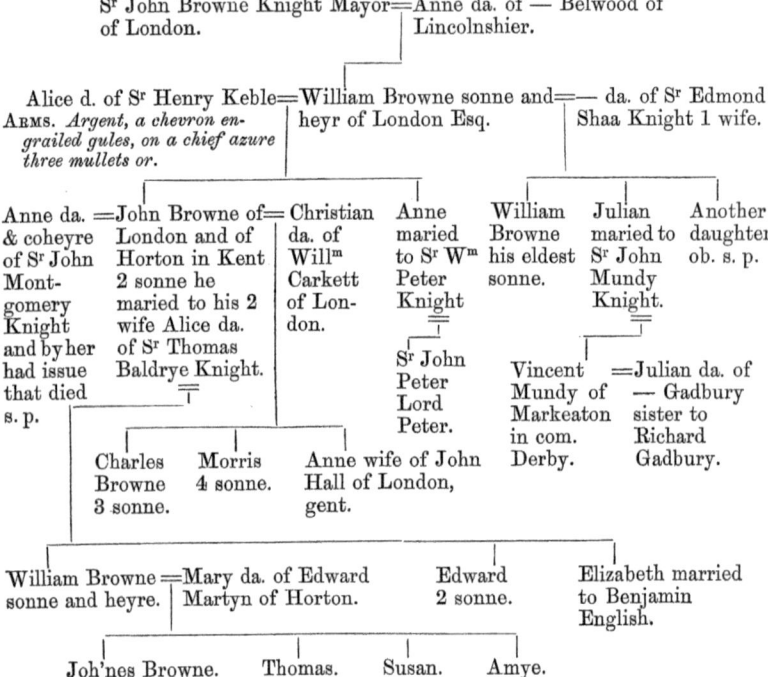

Sᵣ John Browne Knight Mayor=Anne da. of — Belwood of
of London. │ Lincolnshier.

Alice d. of Sᵣ Henry Keble=William Browne sonne and=— da. of Sᵣ Edmond
ARMS. *Argent, a chevron en-* │ heyr of London Esq. │ Shaa Knight 1 wife.
grailed gules, on a chief azure
three mullets or.

Anne da. =John Browne of= Christian   Anne   William   Julian   Another
& coheyre London and of da. of   maried   Browne   maried to   daughter
of Sᵣ John Horton in Kent Willᵐ   to Sᵣ Wᵐ   his eldest Sᵣ John   ob. s. p.
Mont-   2 sonne he   Carkett   Peter   sonne.   Mundy
gomery   maried to his 2 of Lon-   Knight   Knight.
Knight   wife Alice da. don.
and by her of Sᵣ Thomas   Sᵣ John
had issue Baldrye Knight.   Peter   Vincent   =Julian da. of
that died   Lord   Mundy of   — Gadbury
s. p.   Peter.   Markeaton   sister to
                                                    in com.   Richard
            Charles   Morris   Anne wife of John   Derby.   Gadbury.
            Browne   4 sonne. Hall of London,
            3 sonne.   gent.

William Browne =Mary da. of Edward   Edward   Elizabeth married
sonne and heyre. │ Martyn of Horton.   2 sonne.   to Benjamin
                                                    English.

    Joh'nes Browne.   Thomas.   Susan.   Amye.

Barne.

ARMS. *Quarterly :—1 and 4. Azure, three leopards' heads argent. 2 and 3. Argent, a chevron azure between three Cornish choughs sable.*
CREST. *On a mound vert an eagle rising argent, beaked and ducally gorged or.*

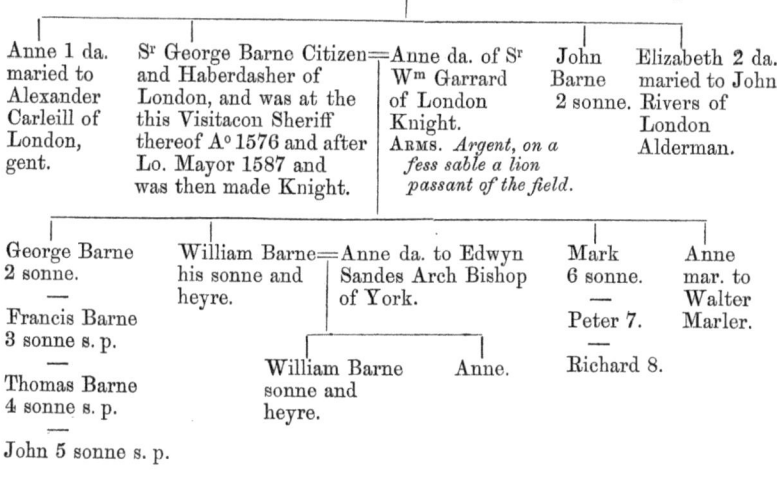

Sir George Barne of London, Knight=Alice da. of Brooke of Shropshier.

Anne 1 da. maried to Alexander Carleill of London, gent.

Sʳ George Barne Citizen and Haberdasher of London, and was at the this Visitacon Sheriff thereof Aᵒ 1576 and after Lo. Mayor 1587 and was then made Knight. =Anne da. of Sʳ Wᵐ Garrard of London Knight. ARMS. *Argent, on a fess sable a lion passant of the field.*

John Barne 2 sonne.

Elizabeth 2 da. maried to John Rivers of London Alderman.

George Barne 2 sonne.
—
Francis Barne 3 sonne s. p.
—
Thomas Barne 4 sonne s. p.
—
John 5 sonne s. p.

William Barne his sonne and heyre. =Anne da. to Edwyn Sandes Arch Bishop of York.

William Barne sonne and heyre.

Anne.

Mark 6 sonne.
—
Peter 7.
—
Richard 8.

Anne mar. to Walter Marler.

Browne.

ARMS. *Or, a chevron engrailed barry wavy argent and azure, between three cranes statant of the last.*
CREST. *A crane statant azure, beaked and legged or, holding in his mouth an ear of barley of the last.*

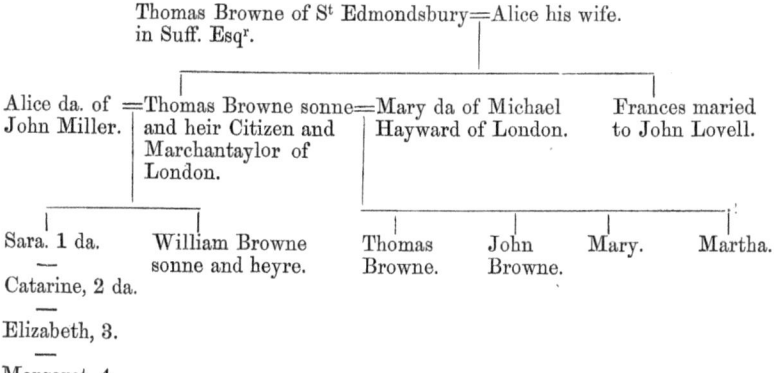

Thomas Browne of Sᵗ Edmondsbury=Alice his wife.
in Suff. Esqʳ.

Alice da. of John Miller. =Thomas Browne sonne and heir Citizen and Marchantaylor of London. =Mary da of Michael Hayward of London.

Frances maried to John Lovell.

Sara. 1 da.
—
Catarine, 2 da.
—
Elizabeth, 3.
—
Margaret, 4.

William Browne sonne and heyre.

Thomas Browne.

John Browne.

Mary.

Martha.

E

Lambert.

ARMS. *Argent, on a bend engrailed between two lions rampant sable, three annulets argent.*
CREST. *A demi-pegasus ermine, with wings expanded ermines.*

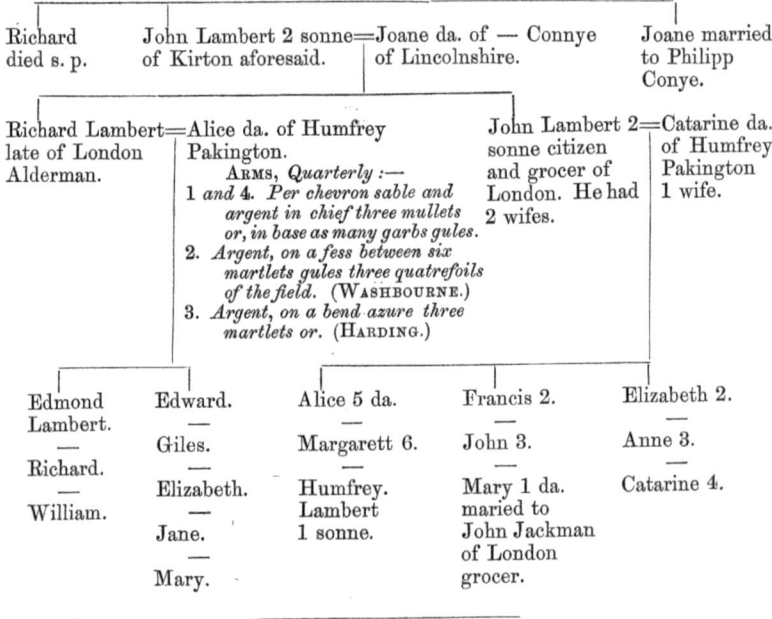

Richard Lambert of Kirton in Holand in com. Lincoln gent.

Richard died s. p.

John Lambert 2 sonne=Joane da. of — Connye of Kirton aforesaid. of Lincolnshire.

Joane married to Philipp Conye.

Richard Lambert=Alice da. of Humfrey late of London Pakington. Alderman.
ARMS, *Quarterly:—*
1 *and* 4. *Per chevron sable and argent in chief three mullets or, in base as many garbs gules.*
2. *Argent, on a fess between six martlets gules three quatrefoils of the field.* (WASHBOURNE.)
3. *Argent, on a bend azure three martlets or.* (HARDING.)

John Lambert 2=Catarine da. sonne citizen of Humfrey and grocer of Pakington London. He had 1 wife. 2 wifes.

Edmond Lambert.
—
Richard.
—
William.

Edward.
—
Giles.
—
Elizabeth.
—
Jane.
—
Mary.

Alice 5 da.
—
Margarett 6.
—
Humfrey. Lambert 1 sonne.

Francis 2.
—
John 3.
—
Mary 1 da. maried to John Jackman of London grocer.

Elizabeth 2.
—
Anne 3.
—
Catarine 4.

Hewes.

ARMS. *Argent, on a bend sable three fish naiant of the field, fins and tails or, in chief a mullet gules.*
CREST. *An elephant's head couped azure bezanté, eared and crowned argent, charged with a mullet or.*

John Hewes of Donyvord in com.=Grace da. of — Waldron. Somersett gent.

William Hewes 1 sonne.
—
Roger 2 sonne.

James Hewes 3=Margaret da. of Robt sonne Citizen Bowser and by her and Grocer of hath issue Rowland London; he his eldest sonne and had two wifes. others.

Dorothy maried to Edward Hensley of Devonshier.

Rowland Hewes sonne.

Geffrey Hewes 2 sonne.

Mary.

Martha.

Rich.

ARMS *Azure, a chevron or between two lions passant argent.*
CREST. *Out of a ducal coronet argent, a demi-lion issuant, tail forked ermine.*

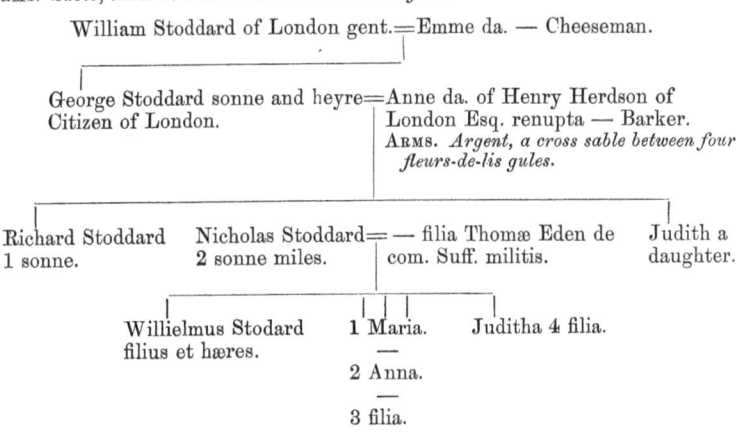

Thomas Riche of Marston in com.=Margery da. of Rafe Done of Flaxyard
Bedf.   in com. Cestr.

1 John Riche sonne=—d. of —   2 William   3 Henry =Mary da. of John Den-
and heyre of London | Kelk of   Riche   Riche   ham of Romsey Abby
gent apothicary to. | Bristoll.   2 sonne.= 3 sonne   in Hampshire.
Q. Eliz. | of London ARMS. *Gules four fusils*
                                              mercer.   *conjoined in fess ermine.*

                              John Riche.

Will'm   Judith vx.   Catherin d. of Thomas=Thomas Rich=Susan d. of Thomas
s. p.   Henry 2   Meade of London   of London,   Reade of St. Ed-
         sone of   Draper 2 wife.   mercer   mund's Bury.
         Henry   ARMS. *Sable, a che-* æt 60–1655.
         Beecher of   *vron between three*
         London   *pelicans vulning*
         Alderman.   *themselves or.*
            =

William.   Edward.   Thomasin 1 yeare   James Rich   Susan Rich
                       old March 1655.   æt 24 1655.   æt 24.

Stoddard.

ARMS. *Sable, three estoiles within a bordure argent.*

William Stoddard of London gent.=Emme da. — Cheeseman.

George Stoddard sonne and heyre=Anne da. of Henry Herdson of
Citizen of London.   London Esq. renupta — Barker.
                                ARMS. *Argent, a cross sable between four*
                                fleurs-de-lis gules.

Richard Stoddard   Nicholas Stoddard=— filia Thomæ Eden de   Judith a
1 sonne.   2 sonne miles.   com. Suff. militis.   daughter.

       Willielmus Stodard   1 Maria.   Juditha 4 filia.
       filius et hæres.   —
                             2 Anna.
                             —
                             3 filia.

𝔓𝔥𝔦𝔩𝔦𝔭𝔭𝔰.

ARMS. *Or, a lion rampant and a chief sable.*
CREST. *A leopard sejant or.*

Thomas Philipps of Tamworth in com. Warr. gen.=Alice da. of Henry Averell.

Henry Phillips sonne and heyre.	William Philips 2 sonne, Citizen & Marchantaylor of London.	=Sibill da. of John Ridley of Ridley. ARMS. *Argent, on a mount vert a bull statant gules.*	Thomas 3 sonne.	Margery maried to Thomas Prise of Coventry. — Joane maried to John Balding.	Alice maried to George Smyth.	Anne maried to John Stuard of Ipswiche. — Margaret maried to William Townrowe of London.

Henry Phillips sonne and heyre.	Alice maried to Michael Fleming 2 sonne to Sr Francis Fleming Knight.	Rachell 2 da.	Anne 3	Mary 4.

𝔅𝔩𝔬𝔲𝔫𝔱.

ARMS. *Quarterly:—1 and 4. Barry nebuly of six, or and sable. 2 and 3. Argent, a lion rampant gules crowned or, within a bordure engrailed sable bezanté, over all a mullet gules.*
CREST. *A lion passant gules crowned or, charged on the breast with a mullet of the last.*

William Blount of Wadeley and Glase=Joyce da. of John Pakington in com. Salop. of Shropshier.

John Blount 1 sonne ob. s. p.	Elizab. da. of Haste= who was first maried to Gage after to Ball of London.	=Thomas Blount= 2 sonne of London Esq.	=Anne da. & heyre of John Cortes of London, Mercer, 1 wife.	Elizabeth maried to Richard Jenkes of the Hay in com. Salop.

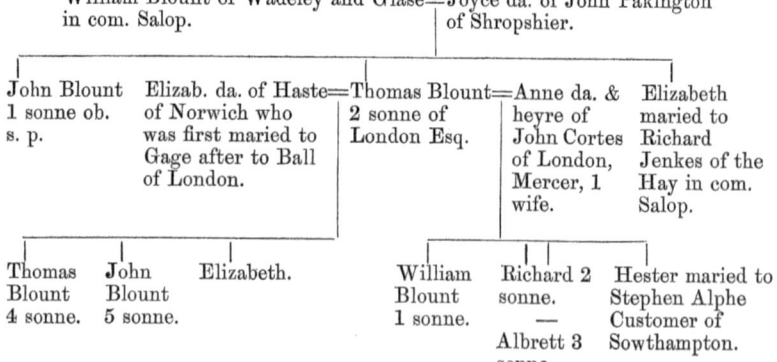

Thomas Blount 4 sonne.	John Blount 5 sonne.	Elizabeth.	William Blount 1 sonne.	Richard 2 sonne. — Albrett 3 sonne.	Hester maried to Stephen Alphe Customer of Sowthampton.

Bowes.

ARMS. *Ermine, three bows bent in pale gules, stringed or, in chief a fleur-de-lis sable for difference.*

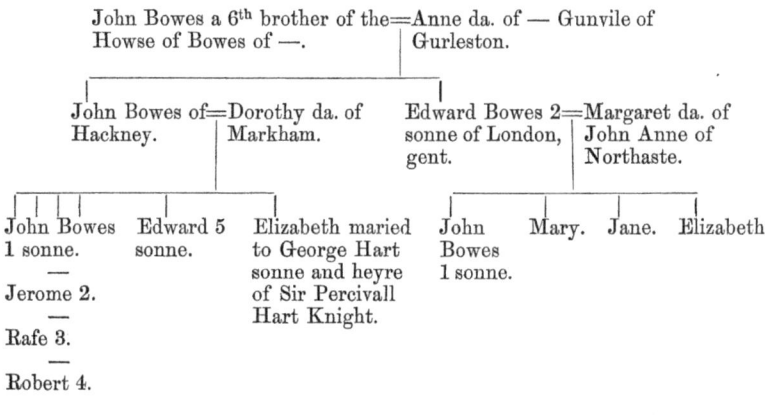

John Bowes a 6th brother of the=Anne da. of — Gunvile of Howse of Bowes of —. Gurleston.

John Bowes of=Dorothy da. of Hackney. Markham.

Edward Bowes 2=Margaret da. of sonne of London, John Anne of gent. Northaste.

John Bowes 1 sonne.
—
Jerome 2.
—
Rafe 3.
—
Robert 4.

Edward 5 sonne.

Elizabeth maried to George Hart sonne and heyre of Sir Percivall Hart Knight.

John Bowes 1 sonne.

Mary.   Jane.   Elizabeth.

Hill.

ARMS. *Sable, a fess ermine between two mountain cats passant guardant argent.*

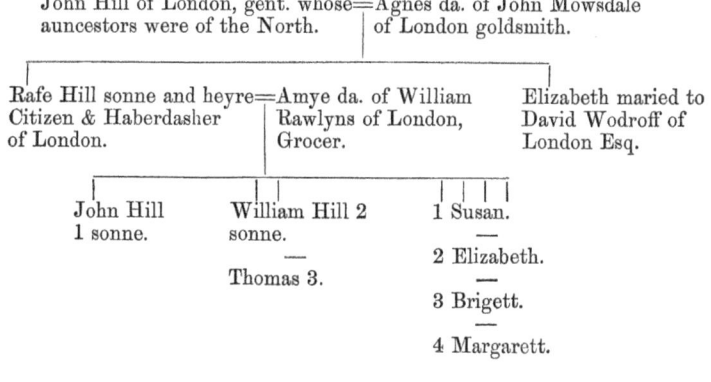

John Hill of London, gent. whose=Agnes da. of John Mowsdale auncestors were of the North. of London goldsmith.

Rafe Hill sonne and heyre=Amye da. of William Citizen & Haberdasher Rawlyns of London, of London. Grocer.

Elizabeth maried to David Wodroff of London Esq.

John Hill 1 sonne.

William Hill 2 sonne.
—
Thomas 3.

1 Susan.
—
2 Elizabeth.
—
3 Brigett.
—
4 Margarett.

Kempe.

ARMS. *Quarterly:—Gules and argent, in the first and last quarters three garbs within a bordure engrailed or, over all a martlet sable for difference.*

Bartholomew Kempe of Gissing in Norff.=— da. of Baron Allen of Bury.

| Robert Kempe 1 sonne. — William 2. — Antony 3 sonne. | Agnes da.= of — Page of Shorn in Kent, gen. | =Edward Kempe= of London mercer 4 sonne. | =Marye da. of Edward Gray of Martyn in Norff. Esq. | Francis 5 sonne. — Bartholmew 6 sonne. | Elizabeth maried to Anthony Throgmorton of Flixon in Suff. |

Robert Kempe.   2 Charles Kemp.   Edmond 3.   Margaret a dawghter.

Staper.

ARMS. *Argent, a cross voided between four estoilles sable.*
CREST. *A lion sejant guardant argent, holding in his paw an estoile sable.*

Richard Staper of London,=Dionise da. of Thomas Hewett
gent.   of London, gent.

Thomas Staper 1   Huett Staper 2   Anne.   Joane.   Mary.
sonne.   sonne.

Biston.

ARMS. *Sable on a bend between six crosses crosslet fitché or, a mullet of the field surmounted by a fleur-de-lis of the second for difference.*

Robert Biston of Belton in com. Lincoln.=

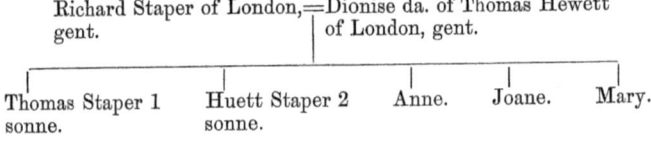

2 wife da. of — =Adam Biston his sonne & heire of = Agnes his 1 wife ob.
London.   s. p.

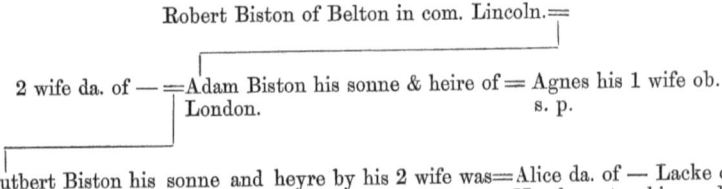

Cutbert Biston his sonne and heyre by his 2 wife was=Alice da. of — Lacke of
Citizen and Girdler of London: he maried to his first   Northamptonshire and as
wife Joane da. of — Stanbridge by whom he had no   yet hath no issue.
issue.

Beckett.

ARMS. *Quarterly :—1. Or, on a chevron between three lions' heads erased gules, a fleur-de-lis between two annulets of the field. 2. Argent, on a fess engrailed gules three crosses crosslet or. 3. Per pale sable and argent, a cross moline counterchanged. 4. Argent, a fess gules between three stags' heads caboshed sable, over all a crescent for difference.*

Anselme Beckett, Citizen and Haberdasher of London.═Anne da. of George Dalton, gent.
ARMS. *Azure semé of crosses crosslet a lion rampant guardant argent.*

William Beckett his sonne and heyre.   Judith.   Sara.   Martha.

Burton.

ARMS. *Argent, on a chevron engrailed between three boars' heads couped sable a bezant.*
CREST. *A boar's head couped or, holding in its mouth a branch vert.*

John Burton of Stapleforth in com. Nott. gent. descended═ of a younger brother of Burton in Yorkshire.

Edmond Burton sonne & heyre Citizen and═Dionise daughter of John Knighton.
Clothworker of London.   ARMS. *Quarterly :—1 and 4. Barry of eight argent and azure, on a canton gules a tun paleways or. 2 and 3. Argent, six annulets—three, two, and one—gules.*

Humphrey Burton 1 sonne & heyre.   James 2 sonne.   3 Edmond.   4 John.   Anne.   Vrsula.   Mary.

Pierson.

ARMS. *Per fess embattled gules and azure, three suns in their splendour or.*
CREST. *A parrot vert, beaked and legged gules.*

Thomas Pierson of Barking in Essex.═ — da. of John Brooke of Ilforde.

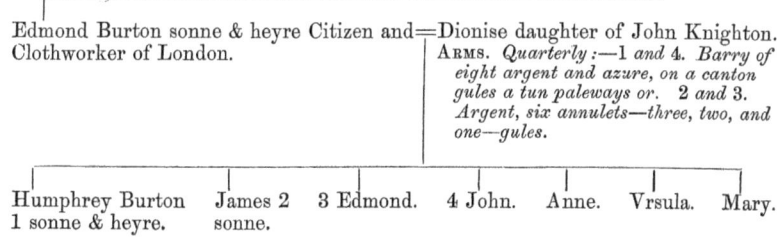

Thomas Pierson of London═Joane da. of Mathew gent.   Gwynne of Wyndesore.   Joane maried to John Frith of Essex.

Joh'nes Pierson sonne & heyre.   Edward 2 sonne.   Mary maried to John Chilestor of London goldsmith.   Elizabeth.   Philip. a da.

Colston.

ARMS. *Quarterly :—1 and 4. Argent, two dolphins haurient respecting each other sable, chained together by their necks, the chain pendent or. 2 and 3. Or, a lion rampant double-queued gules.*

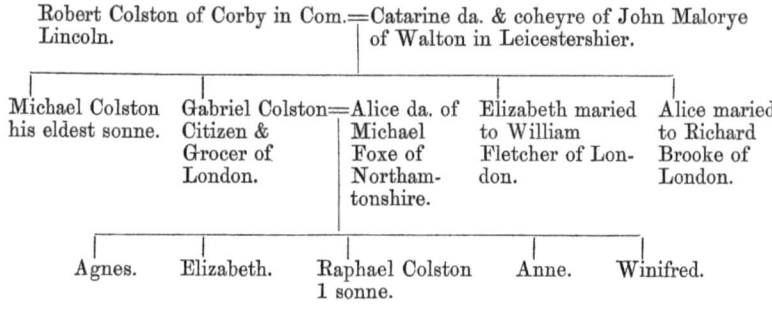

Robert Colston of Corby in Com. Lincoln. = Catarine da. & coheyre of John Malorye of Walton in Leicestershier.

Michael Colston his eldest sonne.

Gabriel Colston Citizen & Grocer of London. = Alice da. of Michael Foxe of Northamtonshire.

Elizabeth maried to William Fletcher of London.

Alice maried to Richard Brooke of London.

Agnes.   Elizabeth.   Raphael Colston 1 sonne.   Anne.   Winifred.

Aldersey.

ARMS. *Gules, on a bend engrailed between two cinquefoils pierced argent three leopards' heads vert.*

Thomas Aldersey Citizen and Haberdasher = Alice da. of Richard Calthrop. of London.

Hogan.

ARMS. *Argent, a chevron engrailed vairy or and gules between three hurts, each charged with a lion's paw erased in bend of the field ; in chief an annulet sable.*
CREST. *A lion's paw couped and erect argent, charged with an annulet sable, holding in its claws another erased gules.*

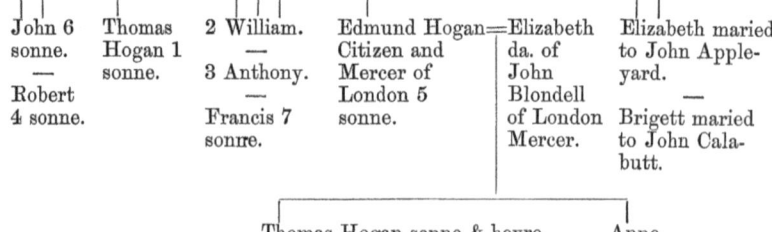

Robert Hogan of East Bradnam in com. Northampt. = Brigitt da. of Sr Richard Fowler of Ricott in com. Oxon.

John 6 sonne. — Robert 4 sonne.

Thomas Hogan 1 sonne. —

2 William. — 3 Anthony. — Francis 7 sonne.

Edmund Hogan Citizen and Mercer of London 5 sonne. = Elizabeth da. of John Blondell of London Mercer.

Elizabeth maried to John Appleyard. — Brigett maried to John Calabutt.

Thomas Hogan sonne & heyre.   Anne.

Conyers.

ARMS. *Azure, a maunch or, in chief a crescent of the second surmounted by another gules.*

CREST. *A sinister wing gules, differenced as the arms.*

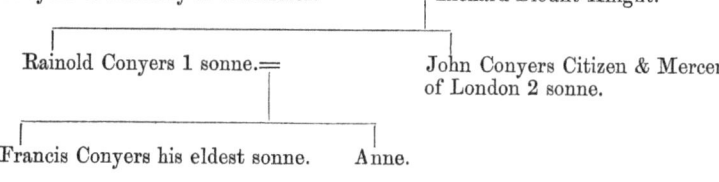

Francis Conyers descended of a younger howse=Anne da. of Blount sister to S[r] of Conyers of Horneby in Yorkshier. | Richard Blount Knight.

Rainold Conyers 1 sonne.= | John Conyers Citizen & Mercer of London 2 sonne.

Francis Conyers his eldest sonne. Anne.

Smythe.

ARMS. *Gules, on a chevron or between three bezants three crosses pattée fitchée, in chief a martlet of the second.*

CREST. *A dexter arm couped at the elbow per pale or and gules, the cuff argent, holding in the hand proper a griffin's head erased azure, beaked and charged with a martlet or.*

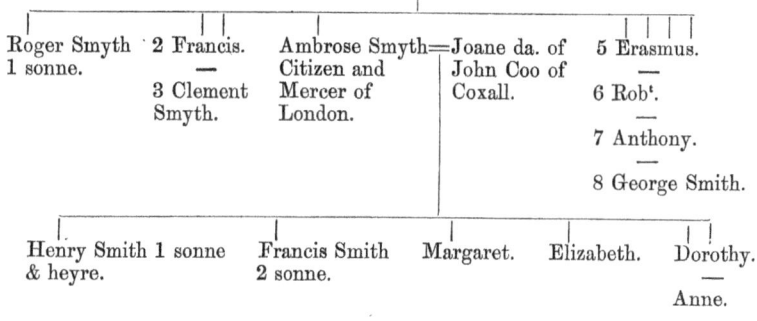

John Hares *alias* Smyth of Withcock=Dorothy da. of Richard Cave of in com. Leic. gent. | Stanford Esq.

Roger Smyth 1 sonne. 2 Francis. — 3 Clement Smyth.

Ambrose Smyth=Joane da. of Citizen and John Coo of Mercer of Coxall. London.

5 Erasmus. — 6 Rob[t]. — 7 Anthony. — 8 George Smith.

Henry Smith 1 sonne & heyre.

Francis Smith 2 sonne.

Margaret. Elizabeth. Dorothy. — Anne.

Candeler.

ARMS. *Argent, three pellets in bend cotised sable between two pellets impaling (for Lock). Quarterly:—1 and 4. Per fess azure and or, a pale counterchanged, in the first three falcons rising and holding in their mouths a padlock of the second. 2 and 3. Sable, a chevron between three conies' heads erased argent.* (SPENCER.)

CREST. *A goat's head couped sable, attired argent.*

Ric. Candeler.= — da. of — Lock.

Holme.

ARMS. *Quarterly :—1 Barry of eight or and azure, on a canton argent, a chaplet gules. 2. Argent, a chevron azure within a bordure engrailed sable. 3. Gules, a cross engrailed argent, in the dexter chief a crescent or. 4. Or, three cocks gules, over all a mullet for difference.*

CREST. *A lion's head couped or, charged with a mullet for difference, ensigned with a cap of maintenance azure, turned up ermine.*

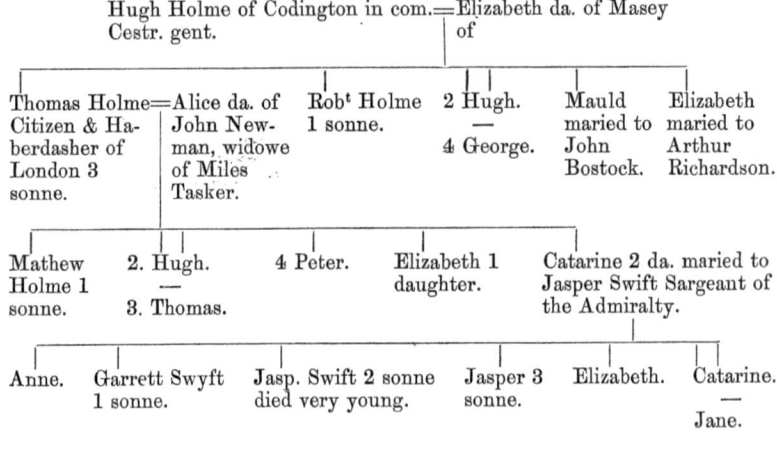

Hugh Holme of Codington in com.=Elizabeth da. of Masey
Cestr. gent. of

Thomas Holme=Alice da. of | Robᵗ Holme | 2 Hugh. | Mauld | Elizabeth
Citizen & Ha- | John New- | 1 sonne. | — | maried to | maried to
berdasher of | man, widowe | | 4 George. | John | Arthur
London 3 | of Miles | | | Bostock. | Richardson.
sonne. | Tasker. |

Mathew | 2. Hugh. | 4 Peter. | Elizabeth 1 | Catarine 2 da. maried to
Holme 1 | — | | daughter. | Jasper Swift Sargeant of
sonne. | 3. Thomas. | | | the Admiralty.

Anne. | Garrett Swyft | Jasp. Swift 2 sonne | Jasper 3 | Elizabeth. | Catarine.
| 1 sonne. | died very young. | sonne. | | —
| | | | | Jane.

Saunders.

ARMS. *Per chevron sable and argent, three elephants' heads erased counterchanged, tusked or, a crescent for difference.*

CREST. *An elephant's head erased sable, ears and tusks argent, charged with a crescent for difference.*

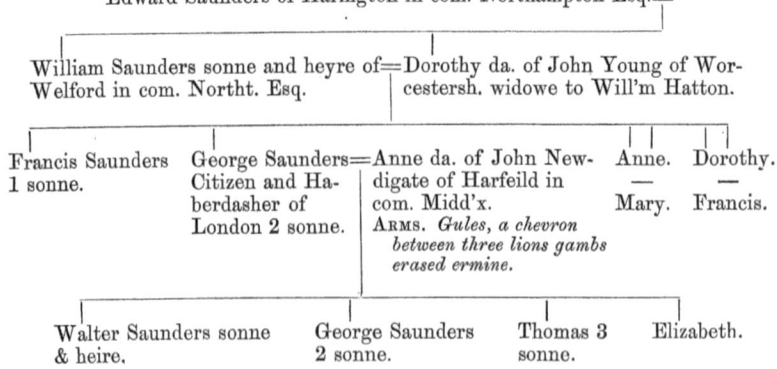

Edward Saunders of Harington in com. Northampton Esq.=

William Saunders sonne and heyre of=Dorothy da. of John Young of Wor-
Welford in com. Northt. Esq. | cestersh. widowe to Will'm Hatton.

Francis Saunders | George Saunders=Anne da. of John New- | Anne. | Dorothy.
1 sonne. | Citizen and Ha- | digate of Harfield in | — | —
| berdasher of | com. Midd'x. | Mary. | Francis.
| London 2 sonne. | ARMS. *Gules, a chevron*
| | *between three lions gambs*
| | *erased ermine.*

Walter Saunders sonne | George Saunders | Thomas 3 | Elizabeth.
& heire. | 2 sonne. | sonne.

𝔚eaber.

ARMS. *Quarterly :—1 and 4. Or, on a fess azure between two cotices gules as many garbs of the field. 2. Azure, on a bend between two cotices argent three escallops gules.* (BOHUN.) *3. Sable, a lion rampant, double queued argent,—over all a crescent for difference.* (WASTNEYS.)

CREST. *An antelope passant ermine, attired or, supporting with the dexter foot an escutcheon or.*

Walter Weaver of Herefordshire Esq.=

Walter Weaver sonne and=Joane da. and heyre of Gilbert Bohun of Shropshier
heyre of Walter. & of Margaret his wife da. & heyre of Tho. Wastneys
of Shropshier Esq.

Walter Weaver sonne & Thomas Weaver 2 sonne.=Margaret da. of Richard
heyre. Wisham Knight.

Walter Weaver.=Mauld da. of John Burghill Esq.

Thomas Weaver.=Anne da. of Delabere.

John Weaver.=Jane da. of James Apleby.

Jenkin Weaver 1=Margarett da. of Robt Griff. 3. Walter. Henry 4 sonne.
sonne. Nanton.

John Weaver Griffith Weaver 2 sonne of Pres-=Ellen da. of Hugh Ellen.
1 sonne. tene in Herefordshier & Rad- John Sadler. 3 sonne.
nock.

John Weaver of London gent. sonne & heire=Alice da. of Thomas Anton, Clarke
of Griffith. of the Wards.

John Weaver sonne Thomas 2 sonne. George 3. James 4. Anne. Catharine.
& heire.

Hodsdon.

ARMS. *Argent, a bend wavy gules between two horseshoes azure.*

CREST. *A man's head proper couped at the shoulders, vested azure, collared or, on the head a cap of maintenance of the last turned up with fur proper.*

Thomas Hodsdon descended of Hodsdon of Hodsdon in Hertfordshier Esq.=

Simon Hodsdon his only sonne of Hodsdon and=Joane da. of John Etheredge of
of Edgeworth in com. Mid. ar.   Edgeworth.

| Nicholas Hodsden 1 sonne duxit filiam Mayne de com. Hertf. | Elizab. da. of=Christopher Wm Blunt of Hodsdon Osbaston in Citizen and comit. Leic. Haber- vidua Saun- dasher of ders. London 2 sonne. | =Alice da. of Alex. Carleill of London. ARMS. *Or, on a cross engrailed gules five martlets of the field, in the first and fourth quarters a rose, in the second and third a griffin's head erased of the second.* | Custance 1 da. ma- ried to Michael Moseley. — Anne maried to Richard Webbe. — Grace maried to Widow of Bucking- hamshier. |

Vrsula sole daughter=Sr John Lee sonne of Tho. Leigh
and heyre.   of Stonley in com. Warr.

Thomas Lee=Mary da. of Sr Thomas Egerton
son to my Lord Chancellor.

| 2 Henry Hoddesdon Rector Eccl'iæ de Iseldon al's Islington Anne da. of Robert Sibthorpe his wife. She was before twise maried first to Richard Martyn after to John Nicholas sonne & heire of Sir Ambrose Nicholas Mayor of Lon- don. | 3 Xpofer Hodsdon Attorney in the King's Bench. | John Hodsdon. = Jane Hay- wood. | Thomas Hoddes- don 4 sonne. = da. of Markes of Sur- rey. | 5 Edward Hodsdon Citizen & Draper of London. = Anne da. of — Richard- son. |

3 Jane.   1 Brigett.   2 Eliz.   John Hodson.   2 Xpofer.

3 Thomas.   4 Edward.

Hartford.

ARMS. *Barry nebulé of six or and azure, on a chief sable three stags' heads caboshed or.*

CREST. *A dexter arm erect couped at the elbow, vested per pale argent and gules, holding in the hand sable a stag's horn.*

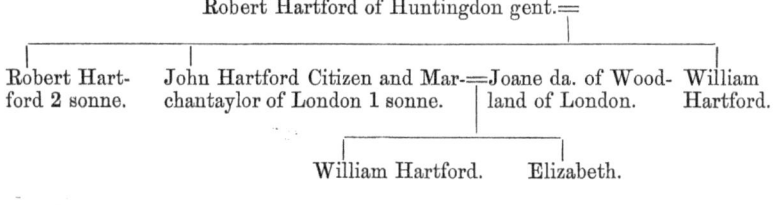

Robert Hartford of Huntingdon gent.⚊

Robert Hartford 2 sonne.

John Hartford Citizen and Marchantaylor of London 1 sonne.⚊Joane da. of Woodland of London.

William Hartford.

William Hartford. Elizabeth.

Heath.

ARMS. *Per chevron sable and or, in chief two mullets pierced of the second, in base a heathcock of the first combed and wattled gules, a crescent of the last for difference.*

CREST. *A heathcock's head erased or, combed and wattled gules, a crescent sable for difference.*

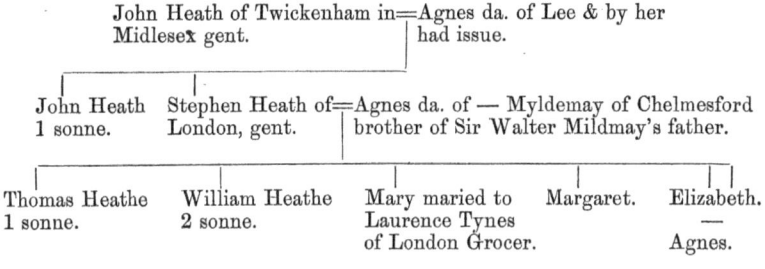

John Heath of Twickenham in Midlesex gent.⚊Agnes da. of Lee & by her had issue.

John Heath 1 sonne.

Stephen Heath of London, gent.⚊Agnes da. of — Myldemay of Chelmesford brother of Sir Walter Mildmay's father.

Thomas Heathe 1 sonne.

William Heathe 2 sonne.

Mary maried to Laurence Tynes of London Grocer.

Margaret.

Elizabeth.
—
Agnes.

Partridge.

ARMS. *Gules, on a bend between two lions rampant or three parrots vert, beaked and legged gules.*

CREST. *Out of a rose gules stalked and leaved vert, a lion's head couped or.*

Anne da. of Fildus 1 wife.⚊Affabel Partridge of London Esq. and Principall goldsmith vnto our Sou'eyne Lady Quene Elizabeth.⚊Margery da. of Gilbard of Sussex.
ARMS. *Argent a talbot passant sable, on a chief indented of the second three besants.*

Thomas Partridge his sonne and heire.

Ellen maried to Thomas Bartellett of London.

Mary maried to Thomas Wadnall of London.

Tuck.

ARMS. *Quarterly :—1 and 4. Argent, on a chevron between three greyhounds' heads erased sable, collared or, as many plates. 2. Per fess or and azure, a lion rampant billetté counterchanged. 3. Or, a cross engrailed gules.*

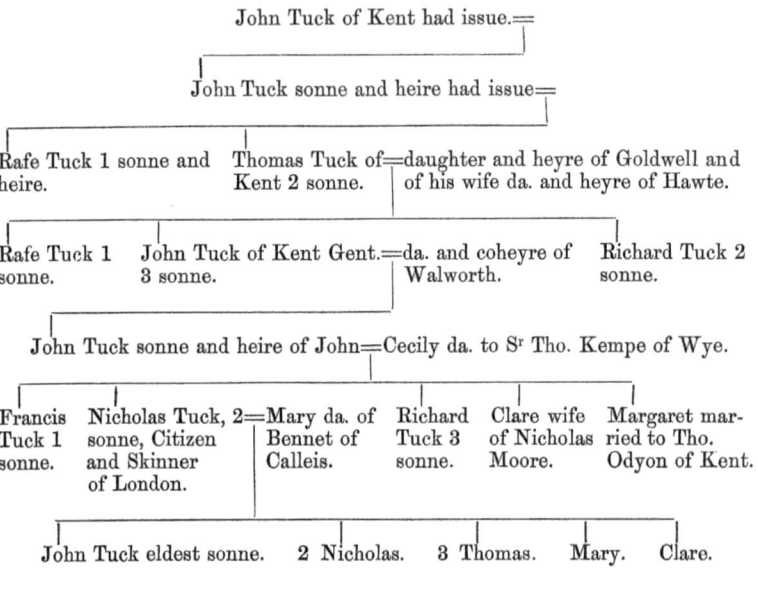

John Tuck of Kent had issue.=

John Tuck sonne and heire had issue=

Rafe Tuck 1 sonne and heire.

Thomas Tuck of=daughter and heyre of Goldwell and
Kent 2 sonne.   of his wife da. and heyre of Hawte.

Rafe Tuck 1 sonne.

John Tuck of Kent Gent.=da. and coheyre of
3 sonne.   Walworth.

Richard Tuck 2 sonne.

John Tuck sonne and heire of John=Cecily da. to Sᵣ Tho. Kempe of Wye.

Francis Tuck 1 sonne.

Nicholas Tuck, 2=Mary da. of
sonne, Citizen   Bennet of
and Skinner   Calleis.
of London.

Richard Tuck 3 sonne.

Clare wife of Nicholas Moore.

Margaret married to Tho. Odyon of Kent.

John Tuck eldest sonne.   2 Nicholas.   3 Thomas.   Mary.   Clare.

Hoskyns.

ARMS. *Per pale gules and azure, a chevron engrailed or, between three lions rampant argent.*

CREST. *A cock's head or pelletté, combed and wattled gules, between two wings expanded of the first.*

Thomas Hoskyns of Monmouth=Jane da. of Catchmade of
in Wales.   Gloucestershire.

Charles Hos-=— daughter of
kyns 1   Inglosse.
sonne.

George Hoskyns 2 sonne.

Joane maried first to John ap
Owen 2 to William Jenkyns 3 to
John Knithlyn.

Inglosse Coate his sonnes wife.
*Barry of six or and azure, on a canton argent
five billets in saltire of the first.*

Gilbert.

ARMS. *Azure, a chevron ermine, between three eagles displayed or.*
CREST. *An eagle displayed azure.*

Richard Gilbert of Somerson in com. Suff. gent.=Anne da. of .... Cortnoll.

| Henry Gilbert 1 sonne. | Henry Gilbert 3=Elizabeth da. of ... Howes. sonne Citizen ARMS. *Argent, a chevron be-* and Goldsmith *tween three wolves' heads* of London. *couped sable.* | Edward=Alice da. of Gilbert Bond of 2 Warwicksh. sonne. |

| Sir John Gilbert of Suff. | Dorothy 1 da. mar. to Sʳ George Speak of Som'stshire. | .... filius objit juvenis. | Elizabeth 1 marr. to .... Colby and after to Sʳ Michael Mollyns of Wallingford in com. Bark. |

Mabbe.

ARMS. *Per pale gules and azure, a tiger passant argent.*
CREST. *A wivern with wings endorsed or pellettée.*

John Mabbe of Clayton in comitatu=Joane da. of ... Goble of
Sussex.   Sussex.

| John Mabbe 1 sonne Citizen=Isabell da. of Richard Colley and goldsmith of London. of Shropshier. | Richard. 2 sonne. | Nicholas. 3 sonne. |

| John Mabbe=Martha da. of London of William gent., 1 Denham of sonne. London. | Richard 2 sonne. | 3. Stephen. — 4. Robᵗ — 5. Edward. — 6. Willᵐ. | Mary mar. to John Dolman. | Susan. | Catarine. |

John Mabbe 1 sonne.   2. William.

Castelyn.

ARMS. *Quarterly :—1 and 4. Sable, on a chevron or between three castles therefrom issuing as many demi-lions argent, three anchors azure. 2 and 3. Or, on a mount vert an eagle displayed sable.*

Castelyn of London gent.=

Heton.

ARMS. *Argent, six trefoils slipped vert.*

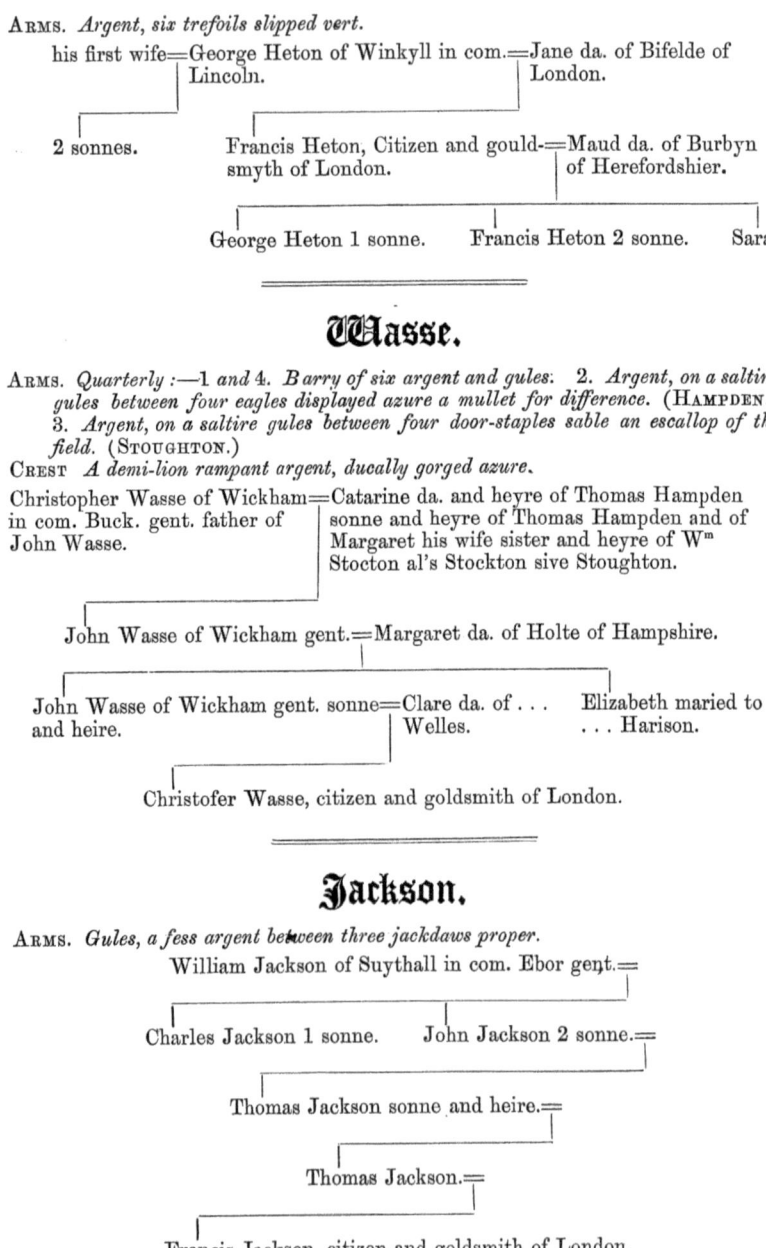

his first wife=George Heton of Winkyll in com.=Jane da. of Bifelde of
     Lincoln.   London.

2 sonnes. Francis Heton, Citizen and gould-=Maud da. of Burbyn
     smyth of London.   of Herefordshier.

George Heton 1 sonne. Francis Heton 2 sonne. Sara.

Wasse.

ARMS. *Quarterly :—1 and 4. Barry of six argent and gules. 2. Argent, on a saltire
gules between four eagles displayed azure a mullet for difference.* (HAMPDEN.)
*3. Argent, on a saltire gules between four door-staples sable an escallop of the
field.* (STOUGHTON.)
CREST *A demi-lion rampant argent, ducally gorged azure.*

Christopher Wasse of Wickham=Catarine da. and heyre of Thomas Hampden
in com. Buck. gent. father of sonne and heyre of Thomas Hampden and of
John Wasse.   Margaret his wife sister and heyre of Wᵐ
          Stocton al's Stockton sive Stoughton.

John Wasse of Wickham gent.=Margaret da. of Holte of Hampshire.

John Wasse of Wickham gent. sonne=Clare da. of . . . Elizabeth maried to
and heire.   Welles.   . . . Harison.

Christofer Wasse, citizen and goldsmith of London.

Jackson.

ARMS. *Gules, a fess argent between three jackdaws proper.*

William Jackson of Suythall in com. Ebor gent.=

Charles Jackson 1 sonne. John Jackson 2 sonne.=

Thomas Jackson sonne and heire.=

Thomas Jackson.=

Francis Jackson, citizen and goldsmith of London.

Gaynsford.

ARMS. *Argent, on a chevron gules between three greyhounds sable, a crescent for difference or.*

CREST. *A demi-maiden couped below the waist, habited gules, crined or, holding in her dexter hand a wreath vert, and in her sinister a rose-branch proper.*

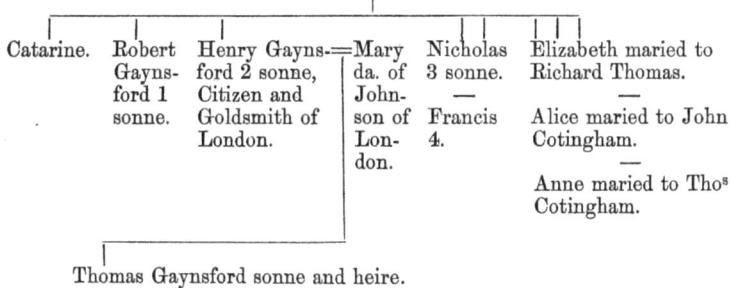

Henry Gaynsford of Cassolton in com.=Catarine da. of — Wilford of London.
Surr. gent.

| Catarine. | Robert Gayns-ford 1 sonne. | Henry Gayns-ford 2 sonne, Citizen and Goldsmith of London. | =Mary da. of Johnson of London. | Nicholas 3 sonne. — Francis 4. | Elizabeth maried to Richard Thomas. — Alice maried to John Cotingham. — Anne maried to Tho[s] Cotingham. |

Thomas Gaynsford sonne and heire.

Muschamp.

ARMS. *Quarterly :—1 and 4. Or, three bars gules, on the first bar a martlet of the field for difference. 2 and 3. Argent, on a chevron gules between three lozenges sable, as many martlets or.*

CREST. *A mountain cat proper, tied round the neck with a scarf argent, charged on the breast with a martlet for difference.*

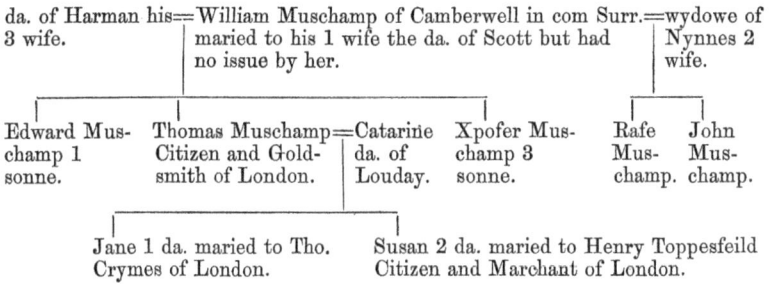

da. of Harman his=   William Muschamp of Camberwell in com Surr.=wydowe of
3 wife. | maried to his 1 wife the da. of Scott but had | Nynnes 2
             | no issue by her. | wife.

| Edward Muschamp 1 sonne. | Thomas Muschamp=Catarine da. of Louday. Citizen and Goldsmith of London. | Xpofer Muschamp 3 sonne. | Rafe Muschamp. | John Muschamp. |

Jane 1 da. maried to Tho.   Susan 2 da. maried to Henry Toppesfeild
Crymes of London.   Citizen and Marchant of London.

G

Metcalfe.

ARMS. *Argent, on a fess vert between three calves sable, a leopard's face between two annulets or.*

CREST. *A demi-sea-calf sable, purfled or.*

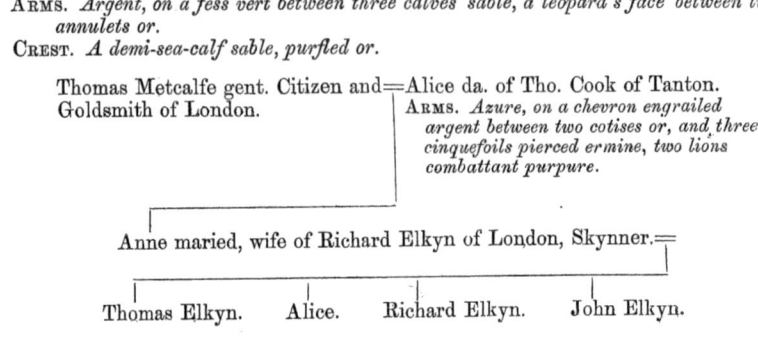

Thomas Metcalfe gent. Citizen and⹀Alice da. of Tho. Cook of Tanton.
Goldsmith of London.

ARMS. *Azure, on a chevron engrailed argent between two cotises or, and three cinquefoils pierced ermine, two lions combattant purpure.*

Anne maried, wife of Richard Elkyn of London, Skynner.⹀

Thomas Elkyn.   Alice.   Richard Elkyn.   John Elkyn.

Gardenor.

ARMS. *Quarterly:—Gules and azure, in the second and third quarters a griffin segreant or, holding in the dexter claw a ring gemmed of the last, over all, on a bend cotised of the last, a leopard's face, holding in the mouth a round buckle between two fleurs-de-lis gules.*

CREST. *A leopard passant argent pelletté, holding in the dexter paw a pineapple or, stalked and leaved vert.*

Thomas Gardenor Citizen and Gouldsmith of London maried to⹀Elizabeth da. of
his 2 wife Beatrix da. of Maye of London.   Tarte.

Thomas Gardenor of Saffron⹀da. of Nicholas Whitney   Richard Gardner
Walden in Essex 1 sonne.   of London.   2 sonne.

Anthony.

ARMS. *Argent, a leopard's head gules between two flaunches sable.*
CREST. *A demi-goat proper, charged with a bezant armed and attired or.*
(ON A SMALL SHIELD.) *"They bore this first."* *Argent, a leopard's head gules between two flaunches sable, on the dexter a rose, on the sinister a mullet or, a crescent in chief for difference.*

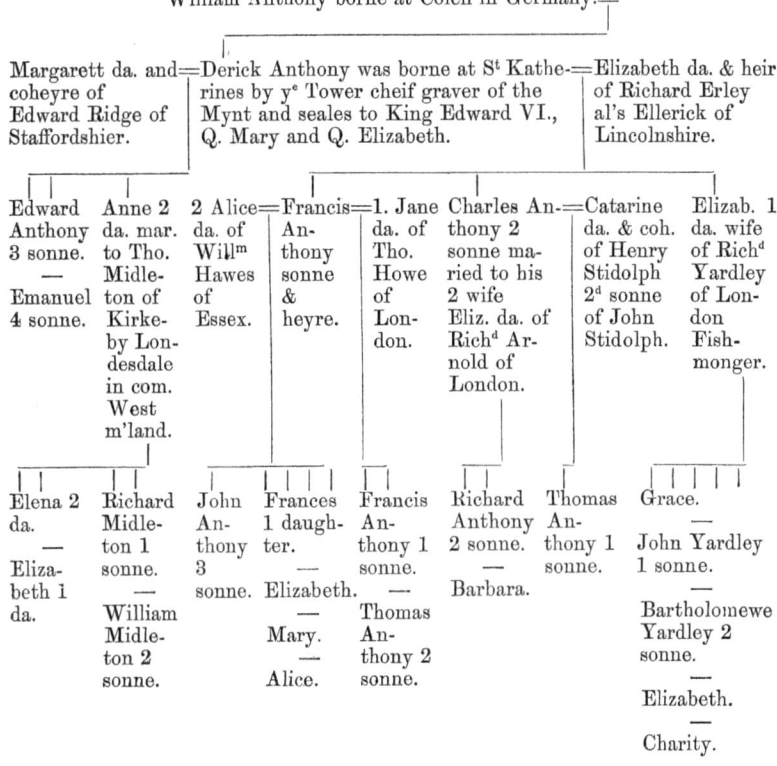

William Anthony borne at Colen in Germany.=

Margarett da. and=Derick Anthony was borne at Sᵗ Kathe-=Elizabeth da. & heir
coheyre of | rines by yᵉ Tower cheif graver of the | of Richard Erley
Edward Ridge of | Mynt and seales to King Edward VI., | al's Ellerick of
Staffordshier. | Q. Mary and Q. Elizabeth. | Lincolnshire.

Edward — Anne 2 — 2 Alice=Francis=1. Jane — Charles An-=Catarine — Elizab. 1
Anthony — da. mar. — da. of | An- | da. of | thony 2 — da. & coh. — da. wife
3 sonne. — to Tho. — Wilⁿ | thony | Tho. | sonne ma- — of Henry — of Richᵈ
— — Midle- — Hawes | sonne | Howe | ried to his — Stidolph — Yardley
Emanuel — ton of — of | & | of | 2 wife — 2ᵈ sonne — of Lon-
4 sonne. — Kirke- — Essex. | heyre. | Lon- | Eliz. da. of — of John — don
— by Lon- — | | don. | Richᵈ Ar- — Stidolph. — Fish-
— desdale — | | | nold of — — monger.
— in com. — | | | London. — —
— West — | | | — —
— m'land. — | | | — —

Elena 2 — Richard — John — Frances — Francis — Richard — Thomas — Grace.
da. — Midle- — An- — 1 daugh- — An- — Anthony — An- — —
— ton 1 — thony — ter. — thony 1 — 2 sonne. — thony 1 — John Yardley
Eliza- — sonne. — 3 — — — sonne. — — — sonne. — 1 sonne.
beth 1 — — — sonne. — Elizabeth. — sonne. — Barbara. — —
da. — William — — — — — — Bartholomewe
— Midle- — — Mary. — Thomas — — — Yardley 2
— ton 2 — — — An- — — — sonne.
— sonne. — — Alice. — thony 2 — — — —
— — — — sonne. — — — Elizabeth.
— — — — — — — —
— — — — — — — Charity.

(Edwardes.)

ARMS. *Argent, a fess ermines between three martlets sable.*
CREST. *A lion's gamb, couped and erect ermine, grasping a goat's leg erased sable, armed or.*

Beneath this coat is written in pencil :—

"It is Edwardes Coate."

Dalton.

ARMS. *Azure semé of crosses crosslet, a lion rampant reguardant argent, charged on the breast with a mullet gules.*

CREST. *A dragon's head vert between two wings or, pelletté.*

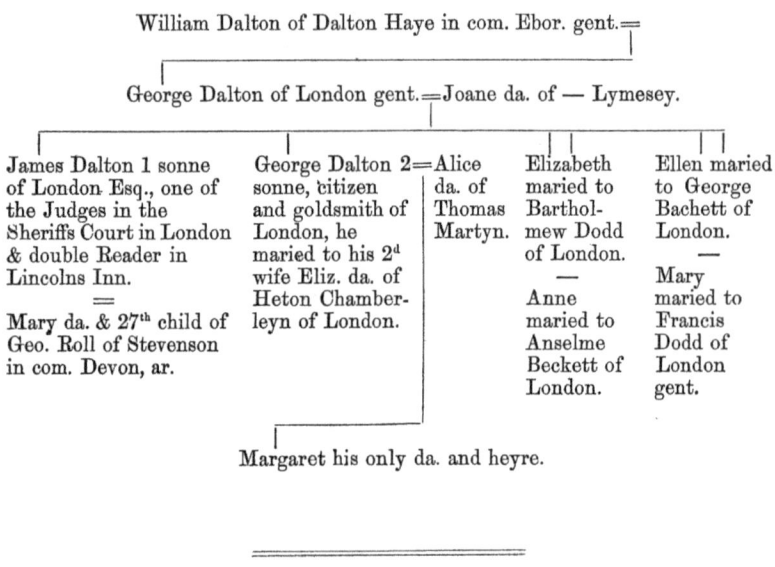

William Dalton of Dalton Haye in com. Ebor. gent.=

George Dalton of London gent.=Joane da. of — Lymesey.

James Dalton 1 sonne of London Esq., one of the Judges in the Sheriffs Court in London & double Reader in Lincolns Inn.

=

Mary da. & 27th child of Geo. Roll of Stevenson in com. Devon, ar.

George Dalton 2=Alice sonne, citizen da. of and goldsmith of Thomas London, he Martyn. maried to his 2d wife Eliz. da. of Heton Chamberleyn of London.

Elizabeth maried to Barthol-mew Dodd of London.

—

Anne maried to Anselme Beckett of London.

Ellen maried to George Bachett of London.

—

Mary maried to Francis Dodd of London gent.

Margaret his only da. and heyre.

Smyth.

ARMS. *Argent, a cross compony counter compony or and azure, between four lions passant sable.*

CREST. *Out of a ducal coronet or a swan close ermine, beaked gules.*

John Smyth of com. Staff. gent.=

Humfrey Smyth sonne & heyre of=Alice da. of — Case of Southampton Gent. Som'settshier.

John Smyth of London, gent.=Mary da. of Sr James Hawes of London Knight.

Carrowe.

ARMS. *Or, three lioncels passant in pale sable, a bordure compony of the same.*
CREST. *A mainmast broken, the round top set off with palisadoes or, headed argent, a lion issuant thereout sable, collared per pale of the first and second.*

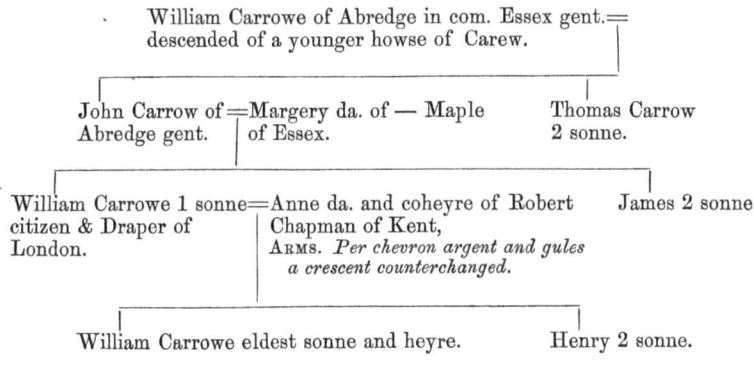

William Carrowe of Abredge in com. Essex gent.=
descended of a younger howse of Carew.

John Carrow of=Margery da. of — Maple   Thomas Carrow
Abredge gent.   of Essex.   2 sonne.

William Carrowe 1 sonne=Anne da. and coheyre of Robert   James 2 sonne.
citizen & Draper of   Chapman of Kent,
London.   ARMS. *Per chevron argent and gules*
     a crescent counterchanged.

William Carrowe eldest sonne and heyre.   Henry 2 sonne.

Pope.

ARMS. *Quarterly 1 and 4. Argent, three popinjays vert, winged or, within a bordure engrailed azure bezanté. 2 and 3. Or, three buckles sable.*
CREST. *A harlequin habited argent and gules, paleways counterchanged, holding in his dexter arm a scimitar of the first, hilted or.*

Francis Pope of London gent. and Draper=Grace da. of Robert Deane
to Queen Elizabeth maried to his 1 wife   of London grocer and
Agnes da. of John Dowse and by her   hath no issue.
had no issue.

Mansbridge.

ARMS. *Quarterly argent and vert, four eagles displayed counterchanged.*

Helen da. of — Warner=John Mansbridge Citizen and=Agnes da.
of London.   Draper of London.   of Abell.

William Mansbridge.   Thomas Mansbridge his eldest sonne.

Luddington.

ARMS. *Quarterly :—1 and 4. Paly of six argent and gules, on a chief of the second a lion passant guardant of the first. 2. Argent, two bars gules, on a canton of the second a cross patonce or.* (KIRKEBY.) *3. Per fess azure and or, a pale counterchanged, on the first three lions rampant of the second* (WHETTILL), *"impaled with Rowe of London."*

Henry Ludyngton gent. first=Joane da. and heyre of William Kirkeby of husband to this Joane, and Kirkeby in Yorkshier which William Kirkeby by her had issue. maried Alice da. & heyre of Whettill. This Joane was after maried to Sʳ William Laxton, Knight.

Nicholas Luddington=Avis his his sonne and heyre wife. Citizen of London.

Joane first maried to — Machell, Sheriff of London, after to Sʳ Thomas Chamberleyne, Knight.

Anne maried to Sʳ Thomas Lodge Knight.

Horspoole.

ARMS. *Sable, on a chevron argent three lions' heads erased of the field.*
CREST. *A demi-pegasus erased, wings expanded ermine, girded round the loins with a ducal coronet or.*

John Horspoole of London, gent.=Hawis da. of — Baker.

Symon Horspoole citizen and=Elizabeth da. of John Smyth of Draper of London. Cossam in com. Wiltesh.

William Horspoole 1 sonne. 2 Simon. 3 Thomas. Elizabeth. Mary. Hawis.

Hodgeson.

ARMS. *Gules, three scimitars in pale argent, hilted gules, the points of the first and third and the hilt of the second to the dexter side, within a bordure engrailed argent pelletté.*
CREST. *A dexter arm erect, couped at the elbow, habited bendy sinister of four argent and gules, holding in the hand proper a covered cup or.*

Thomas Hodgeson of Yorkeshier gent.=Agnes da. of Robert Cooke of Essex.

William Hodgson, citizen and Merchant=Elizabeth da. of Fowke Wall taylor of London. of Cradeley in Shropshire.

Parker.

ARMS. *Argent, a chevron gules between three mullets sable, on a chief azure three stags' heads caboshed of the field.*
CREST. *A reindeer's head erased per fess argent and gules, attired or.*

John Parker of Dantrey in com Northampton=Margery da. of Vincent Crosse
gent. descended of Parker of Norton in   of Warwickshier.
com. Ebor.

William Parker his sonne and heyre.=Margery da. of William Allen of London.

Pullison.

[ARMS. *Per pale argent and sable, three lions rampant counterchanged.*
CREST. *Out of a ducal coronet gules a demi-peacock, wings expanded or.*]

Sr Thomas Pullison Knight Sheriff and after Mayor of London.=

Brett.

ARMS. *Argent semé of crosses crosslet fitché, a lion rampant gules.*

Alexander Brett of Whitstanton in com. Deuon= — da. of Rosemaderos.

John Brett 1   Robert Brett of=Elizabeth da. of Edward Bush of   Symon Brett
sonne.   Lincolnshier   Sison 3 brother to the Bushes of   2 sonne.
         gent.   Hohum.

Robert Brett 1 sonne=Elizabeth da. of Reginald Highgate   Margaret wife of
Citizen & Mar-   of Essex.   — Veale of Lanca-
chantaylor of   ARMS. *Gules, two bars argent, over all*   shier.
London.   *on a bend or a torteau between two*
               leopards' heads azure.

John Brett his   2 William.   3 Robert.   4 Richard.   Elizabeth.   Catharine.
eldest sonne.

Albaney.

ARMS. *Ermine, on a fess between three cinquefoils gules, a greyhound courant or.*
CREST. *Out of a ducal coronet gules, a dolphin embowed argent, purfled or.*

William Albaney of London gent. & Marchantaylor, he=Thomas da. of Richard
maried to his 2 wife Joane da. of Robert Cordall of | Buttle of London.
London.

Francis Albany 1 sonne.	William Albany 2 sonne.	Robert 3 sonne.	1. Mary. 2. Judith.

Bragden.

ARMS. *Argent, a lion passant azure between three fleurs-de-lis gules.*
CREST. *A boar issuant out of a rock proper.*

John Bragden of London gent.=Margery da. of Thomas Body of Worcester.
ARMS. *Argent, on a fess azure three pelicans vulning themselves or.*

Thomas Brogden 1 sonne & heyre.	2 Edward.	3 Richard.	4 William.	Avis maried to Nicholas Tetlowe of London. Mary.

Farrington.

ARMS. *Quarterly :—1 and 4. Argent, a chevron gules between three leopards' heads
  purpure.   2 and 3. Gules, three cinquefoils argent.*
CREST. *A wivern sans wings, tail extended vert.*

John Farrington of Sussex descended of a younger howse=Margaret his wife.
of Farrington in com. Lanc.

John Farrington=Alice da. of Sr Citizen & Cloth-worker of London.	George a preist 2 sonne.	Richard Faring-ton 3 sonne Alderman of London 1609.	Sibill. wife of — Co- vert.	Mary ma-ried to William Danser.
Alexander Faring-ton 1 sonne.	2 John. 3 Thomas.	Elizabeth.	Mirabell.	Marye mar. to — Martindale.

Lucar.

ARMS. *Quarterly :—1 and 4. Argent, a chevron sable between three nags' heads erased gules, bridled or. 2 and 3. Argent, a fess nebulé azure, in chief a lion's head erased of the last between two mascles and one in base gules.*

CREST. *A dexter arm couped at the elbow, vested per pale azure and gules, holding in the hand proper a lure argent, stringed of the second, ringed and knotted or.*

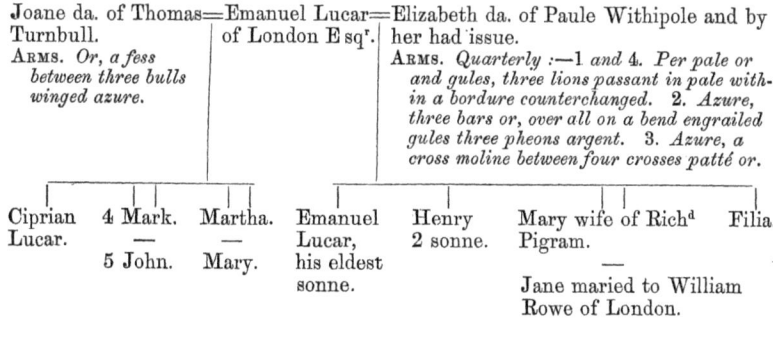

Joane da. of Thomas=Emanuel Lucar=Elizabeth da. of Paule Withipole and by
Turnbull. | of London E sq'. | her had issue.

ARMS. *Or, a fess between three bulls winged azure.*

ARMS. *Quarterly :—1 and 4. Per pale or and gules, three lions passant in pale within a bordure counterchanged. 2. Azure, three bars or, over all on a bend engrailed gules three pheons argent. 3. Azure, a cross moline between four crosses patté or.*

| Ciprian Lucar. | 4 Mark. — 5 John. | Martha. — Mary. | Emanuel Lucar, his eldest sonne. | Henry 2 sonne. | Mary wife of Richd Pigram. — Jane maried to William Rowe of London. | Filia. |

Prowze.

ARMS. *Quarterly of six :—1 and 6. Argent, three lions rampant sable. 2. Argent, a bend gules, on a chief vert two cinquefoils or. 3. Azure, a bend per bend indented gules and argent between six escallops or. (CREWYS.) 4. Argent, a fess dancetté in chief two martlets sable. 5. Azure, a chevron argent between three pears or. (CALMADY.)*

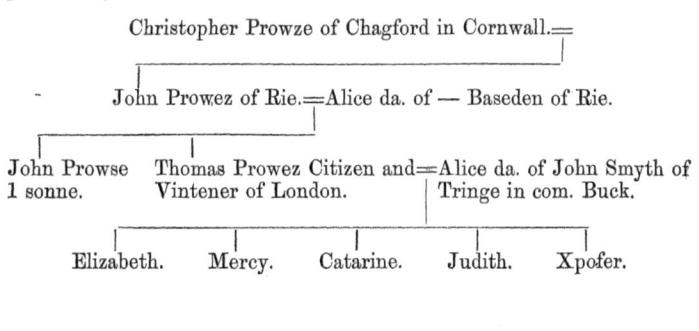

Christopher Prowze of Chagford in Cornwall.=

John Prowez of Rie.=Alice da. of — Baseden of Rie.

| John Prowse 1 sonne. | Thomas Prowez Citizen and=Alice da. of John Smyth of Vintener of London. | Tringe in com. Buck. |

| Elizabeth. | Mercy. | Catarine. | Judith. | Xpofer. |

H

𝔥illes.

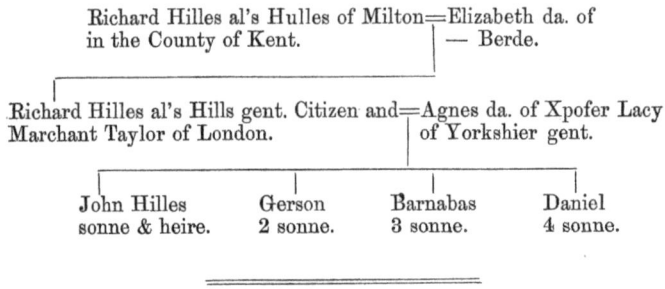

Richard Hilles al's Hulles of Milton=Elizabeth da. of
in the County of Kent. | — Berde.

Richard Hilles al's Hills gent. Citizen and=Agnes da. of Xpofer Lacy
Marchant Taylor of London. | of Yorkshier gent.

| John Hilles sonne & heire. | Gerson 2 sonne. | Barnabas 3 sonne. | Daniel 4 sonne. |

𝔥all.

ARMS. *Argent semé of crosses crosslet, three talbots' heads erased sable.*

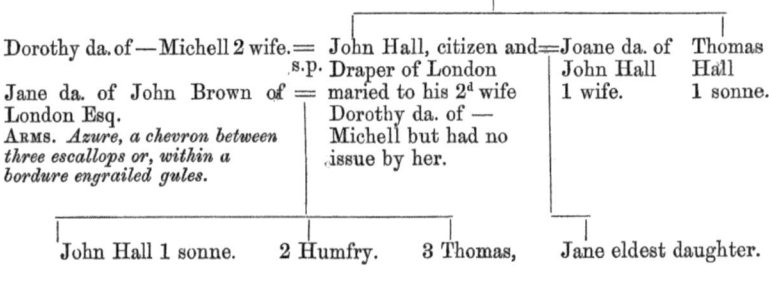

Thomas Hall of Warnam in the County of Sussex.=Margaret da. of Pawthorne.

Dorothy da. of — Michell 2 wife.= John Hall, citizen and=Joane da. of Thomas
s.p. Draper of London John Hall Hall
Jane da. of John Brown of = maried to his 2ᵈ wife 1 wife. 1 sonne.
London Esq. Dorothy da. of —
ARMS. *Azure, a chevron between* Michell but had no
three escallops or, within a .issue by her.
bordure engrailed gules.

| John Hall 1 sonne. | 2 Humfry. | 3 Thomas, | Jane eldest daughter. |

𝔥all.

ARMS. *Argent, a fess between two greyhounds courant sable.*
CREST. *Out of a ducal coronet or, a demi-greyhound sable collared of the first.*

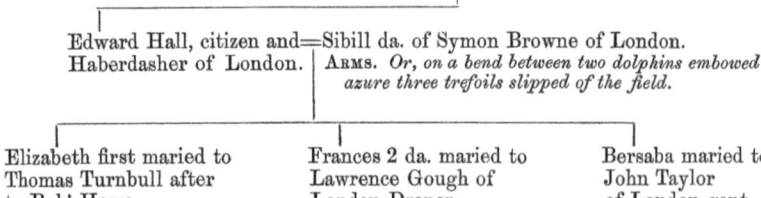

John Hall of Skipton in Craven in Yorkshier.=Alice da. of Merslinge of Kent.

Edward Hall, citizen and=Sibill da. of Symon Browne of London.
Haberdasher of London. | ARMS. *Or, on a bend between two dolphins embowed*
azure three trefoils slipped of the field.

| Elizabeth first maried to Thomas Turnbull after to Robᵗ Howe. | Frances 2 da. maried to Lawrence Gough of London Draper. | Bersaba maried to John Taylor of London gent. |

Rivell.

ARMS. *Per pale indented argent and sable, a chevron gules.*

Robert Rivell of Kellingesbery in com.=Catarine da. of John Russell of
Northt. | London.

Nicholas Rivell Citizen and grocer of London.=Audrey da. of John Michenar.

Robert Rivell sonne & heyre.   Emme.

Jenkynson.

ARMS. *Azure, a fess wavy argent, in chief three estoiles or.*
CREST. *A seahorse assurgent per pale or and azure, crined gules.*

Anthony Jenkynson Citizen and Mercer=Judith da. of John Marshe of
of London. | London Esq.

Alice 1 da.   Mary 2 da.

Marbury.

ARMS. *Quarterly of 9:—1. Sable, a cross engrailed between four pheons argent.*
(MARBURY.) *2. Or, on a fess engrailed azure three garbs of the field.* (MER-
BURY.) *3. Barry nebulé of six or and sable.* (BLOUNT.) *4. (Argent), two
wolves passant in pale (sable), on a bordure (gules) eight saltires couped (or).*
(AYALA.) *5. Or, a four-towered castle azure.* (CASTILE.) *6. Vair.* (BEAU-
CHAMP.) *7. Argent, three fleurs-de-lis azure. 8. Argent, a fess and in chief
three covered cups gules. 9. Vert, a saltire engrailed argent.* (HAWLEY.)

William Merbury father of=Agnes da. & coheyre of Thomas Blount younger
Robert and Thomas | brother to Sr William Blount, and of his wife
Marbury. | the da. & heyre of John Hawley.

Thomas Marbury Citizen &=Agnes da. of — Lynne   Robert Marbury 1
haberdasher of London. | of Northampton.   sonne.

Christian | Humfrey Mar-=Anne da. of Alder-   Anne 1st maried | Alice wife of
maried to | bury 2 sonne | man Bankes of   to — Bradley | Tho. Mar-
Francis | Citizen & | London.   after to Armiger | bury.
Withers. | haberdasher | ARMS. *Sable, on a*   Wade. | —
— | of London. | *cross or between*   — | Elizabeth
Joh'nes | | *four fleurs-de-lis*   Thomasin maried | maried to
Marbery. | | *argent five*   to Thomas | Richards
| | *ogresses.*   Jennyns. | Ellis.

Jenkenson.

James Jenkensonne of Tourley in the=Elen daughter of — Danell of Kedsnape
County of Lankersheyer.   in the County of Lancas‌ʳ.

Robartt Jenkenson of Tourley.=Brigett Whinyard of London.

Sʳ Roburtt Jenkenson=Ann Mary Lee daughter of Sʳ Rob. Lee of Billesley in
of Walcott in the   Worwickshyer 2 sonne of Sʳ Robᵗ Lee, Maior of London
County of Oxford.   by Anne daughter of Sʳ Th. Loe of Lond. Knight.

Coleclogh.

Arms. *Quarterly :—1 and 4. Argent, five eagles displayed in cross sable. 2 and 3.
Sable, a fess between three martlets argent* (Lockwood); *over all a crescent
for difference.*
Crest. *A demi-eagle displayed sable, charged on the breast with a crescent or.*

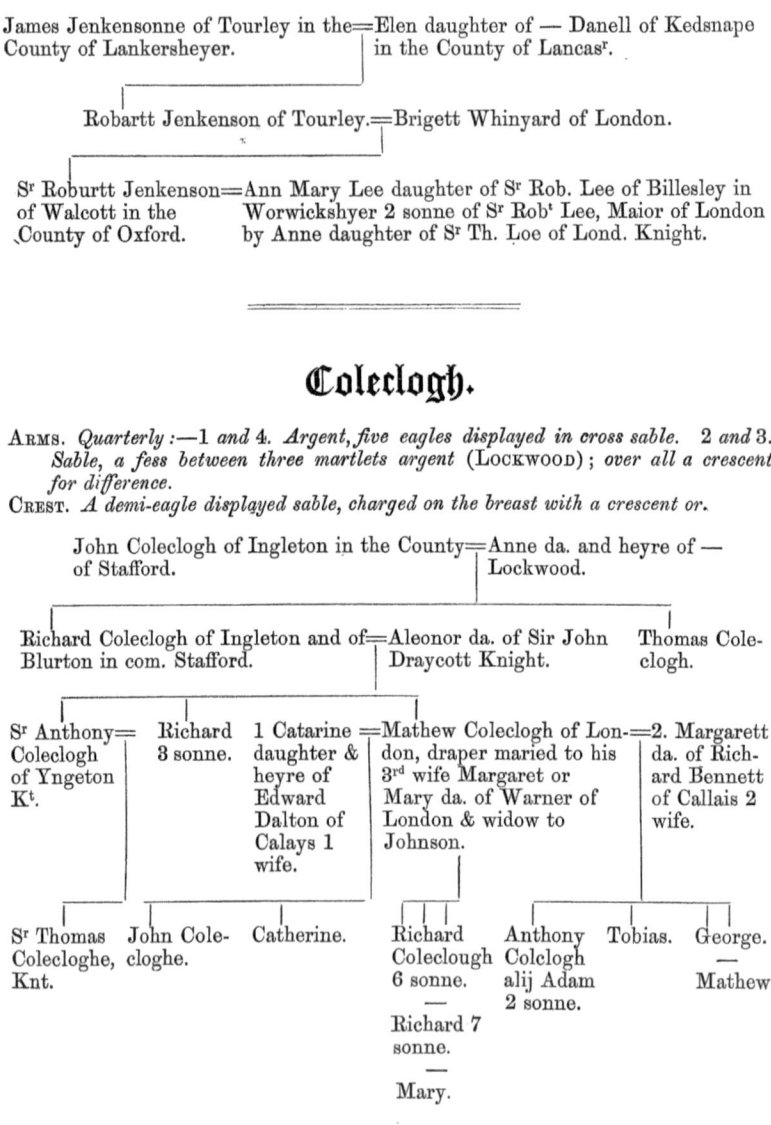

John Coleclogh of Ingleton in the County=Anne da. and heyre of —
of Stafford.   Lockwood.

Richard Coleclogh of Ingleton and of=Aleonor da. of Sir John   Thomas Cole-
Blurton in com. Stafford.   Draycott Knight.   clogh.

Sʳ Anthony= Richard   1 Catarine =Mathew Coleclogh of Lon-=2. Margarett
Coleclogh   3 sonne.   daughter &   don, draper maried to his   da. of Rich-
of Yngeton   heyre of   3ʳᵈ wife Margaret or   ard Bennett
Kᵗ.   Edward   Mary da. of Warner of   of Callais 2
              Dalton of   London & widow to   wife.
              Calays 1   Johnson.
              wife.

Sʳ Thomas   John Cole-   Catherine.   Richard   Anthony   Tobias.   George.
Colecloghe,   cloghe.   Coleclough   Colclogh   —
Knt.   6 sonne.   alij Adam   Mathew.
                                —   2 sonne.
                              Richard 7
                              sonne.
                              —
                              Mary.

Allen.

ARMS. *Quarterly :—1 and 4. Per fess gules and sable, a chevron rompu ermine between three griffins' heads erased argent. 2 and 3. Sable, a chevron ermine between three unicorns' heads erased argent.* (HEDD.)

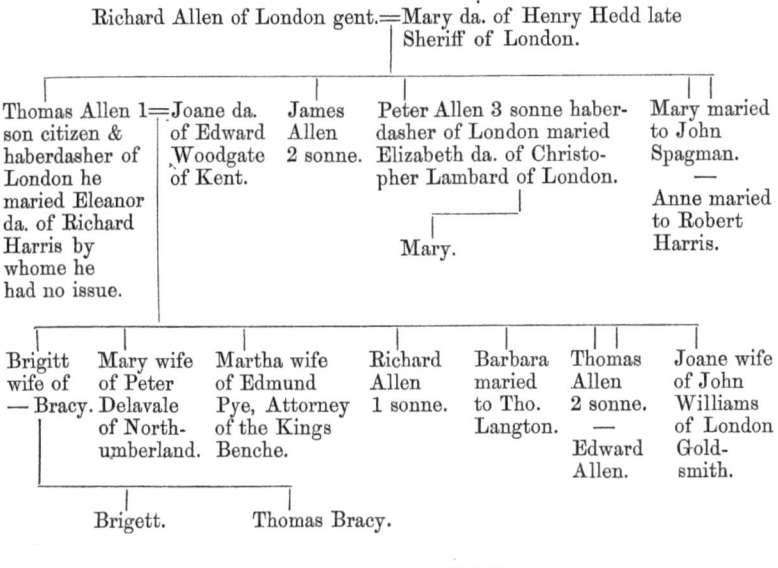

Richard Allen of London gent.=Mary da. of Henry Hedd late Sheriff of London.

Thomas Allen 1=Joane da. of Edward Woodgate of Kent. son citizen & haberdasher of London he maried Eleanor da. of Richard Harris by whome he had no issue.

James Allen 2 sonne.

Peter Allen 3 sonne haberdasher of London maried Elizabeth da. of Christopher Lambard of London.

Mary.

Mary maried to John Spagman.

Anne maried to Robert Harris.

Brigitt wife of — Bracy.

Mary wife of Peter Delavale of Northumberland.

Martha wife of Edmund Pye, Attorney of the Kings Benche.

Richard Allen 1 sonne.

Barbara maried to Tho. Langton.

Thomas Allen 2 sonne. — Edward Allen.

Joane wife of John Williams of London Goldsmith.

Brigett.

Thomas Bracy.

Witton.

ARMS. *Quarterly :—1 and 4. Sable, a water-bouget argent, in chief three bezants. 2 and 3. Argent, a fess gules between three bulls' heads couped sable.*
CREST. *An owl argent, legged sable, ducally gorged or.*

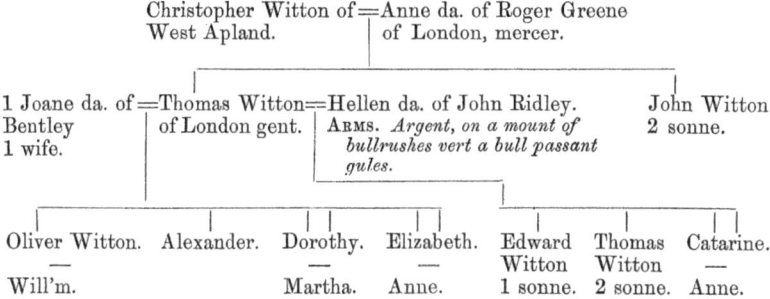

Christopher Witton of West Apland.=Anne da. of Roger Greene of London, mercer.

1 Joane da. of Bentley 1 wife.=Thomas Witton=Hellen da. of John Ridley. of London gent. | ARMS. *Argent, on a mount of bullrushes vert a bull passant gules.*

John Witton 2 sonne.

Oliver Witton. — Will'm.

Alexander.

Dorothy. — Martha.

Elizabeth. Anne.

Edward Witton 1 sonne.

Thomas Witton 2 sonne.

Catarine. — Anne.

𝕳𝖆𝖗𝖉𝖎𝖓𝖌.

ARMS. *Gules, three greyhounds courant in pale or, collared azure.*
CREST. *A demi-leopard rampant ermine, gorged with a collar azure bezanté, chain compony, counter-compony of the last.*

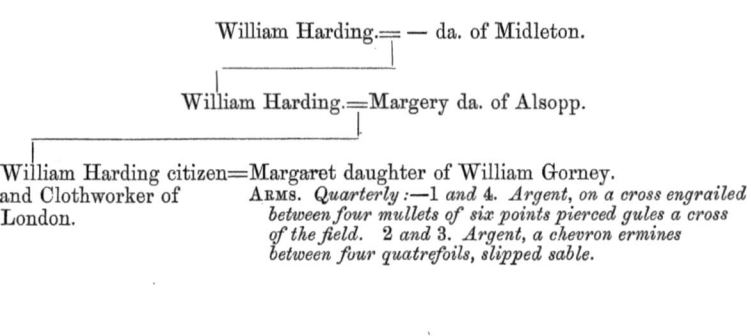

William Harding.═ — da. of Midleton.

William Harding.═Margery da. of Alsopp.

William Harding citizen═Margaret daughter of William Gorney.
and Clothworker of   ARMS. *Quarterly:—1 and 4. Argent, on a cross engrailed*
London.   *between four mullets of six points pierced gules a cross*
                    of the field. 2 and 3. Argent, a chevron ermines
                    between four quatrefoils, slipped sable.

𝕽𝖊𝖉𝖒𝖆𝖓.

ARMS. *Gules, three cushions ermine, tasselled or, in chief a fleur-de-lis of the last for difference.*

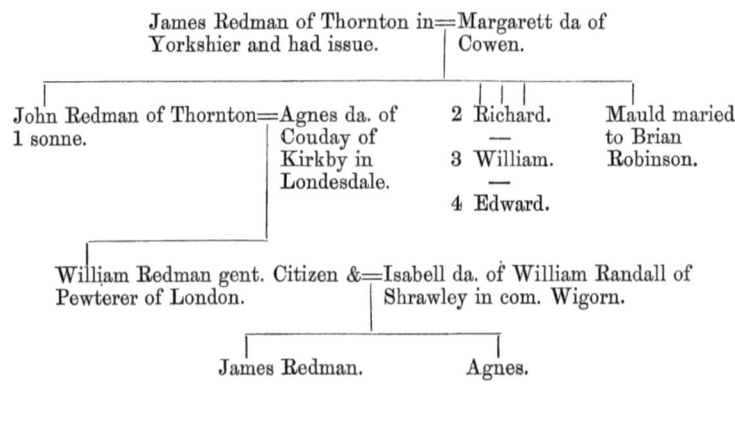

James Redman of Thornton in═Margarett da of
Yorkshier and had issue.   Cowen.

John Redman of Thornton═Agnes da. of   2 Richard.   Mauld maried
1 sonne.   Couday of   —   to Brian
                    Kirkby in   3 William.   Robinson.
                    Londesdale.   —
                                  4 Edward.

William Redman gent. Citizen &═Isabell da. of William Randall of
Pewterer of London.   Shrawley in com. Wigorn.

James Redman.   Agnes.

Dale.

ARMS. *Sable, on a chevron or between three cranes rising argent seven torteaux.*

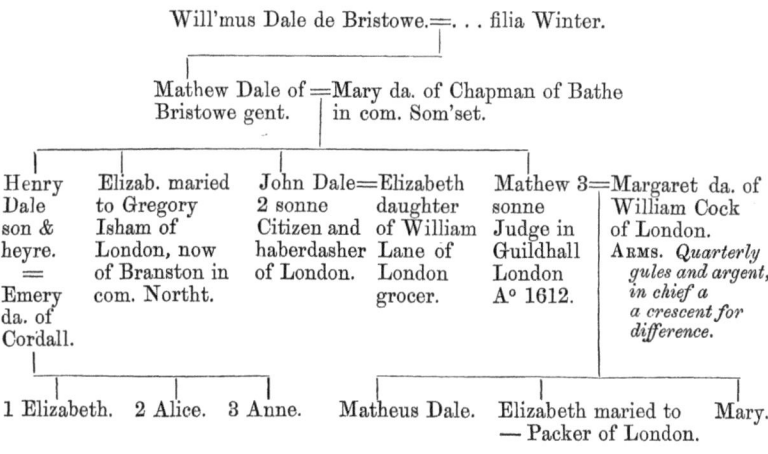

Will'mus Dale de Bristowe.=... filia Winter.

Mathew Dale of =Mary da. of Chapman of Bathe
Bristowe gent. | in com. Som'set.

| Henry Dale son & heyre. = Emery da. of Cordall. | Elizab. maried to Gregory Isham of London, now of Branston in com. Northt. | John Dale=Elizabeth 2 sonne daughter Citizen and of William haberdasher Lane of of London. London grocer. | Mathew 3=Margaret da. of sonne William Cock Judge in of London. Guildhall ARMS. *Quarterly* London *gules and argent,* A° 1612. *in chief a a crescent for difference.* |

1 Elizabeth.   2 Alice.   3 Anne.   Matheus Dale.   Elizabeth maried to   Mary.
— Packer of London.

Erdeswick.

ARMS. *Quarterly of six* :—1. *Argent, on a chevron gules five bezants.* 2. *Argent, a chevron between three eagles' heads erased sable.* 3. *Or, a chevron gules.* 4. *Gules, a fess between six crosses crosslet within a bordure or.* 5. *Or, two bends compony argent and gules.* 6. *Gules, a chevron wavy between three stags' heads caboshed argent.*
CREST. *Out of a ducal coronet gules a boar's head per pale argent and sable.*

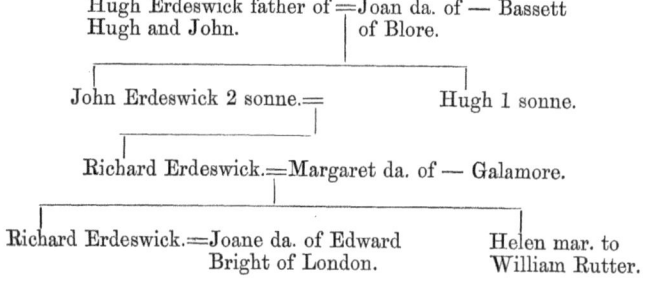

Hugh Erdeswick father of =Joan da. of — Bassett
Hugh and John. | of Blore.

John Erdeswick 2 sonne.=   Hugh 1 sonne.

Richard Erdeswick.=Margaret da. of — Galamore.

Richard Erdeswick.=Joane da. of Edward   Helen mar. to
Bright of London.   William Rutter.

Bramstone.

ARMS. *Or, on a fess sable three plates.*
CREST. *A tun fessways or, thereon a raven sable holding in his beak a carnation-branch proper.*

Hugh Bramstone of London, gent.═Elizabeth da. of — Norris of London.

John Bramstone, citizen &═Margaret daughter	Thomas	Agnes maried to
Mercer of London he	of Thomas	2 sonne.	Xpofer Campion
maried to his 2 wife	Symonds of	of London,
Elizabeth da. of William	London.	mercer.
Chambers.

Roger Bramstone	Elizabeth maried	Grace maried to	Anne 3 daughter.
his only sonne.	to George Buck.	George Selye.

Holland.

ARMS. *Azure, a lion rampant guardant between four crosses patté argent.*

Robert Holland, gentleman.═

John Holland of═Helenor da. of — Shurley	Will'm.	Henry.	Joane.
Surrey, gent.	of Surrey.

William Holland, Citizen and═Elizabeth da. of Robᵗ Bolt
Mercer of London. | of London, mercer.

William Holland 1 sonne.	2 Thomas.	3 Richard.	Joane.	Mary.

Lee.

ARMS. *Argent, on a fess between three leopards' heads sable a crescent or.*

Thomas Lee of Enfeild in═Margarett da. of — Poyner
Staffordshier, gent. | of Strochley.

Richard Lee	Thomas Lee, 2 sonne Citizen═Mary da. of John Holmden.
1 sonne.	and grocer of London.	ARMS. *Sable, a fess between two chevrons ermine.*

Walton.

ARMS. *Argent, on a fleur-de-lis gules, a mullet or.*

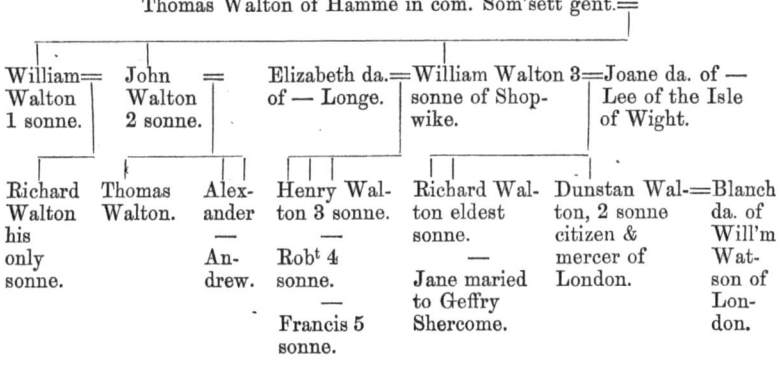

Thomas Walton of Hamme in com. Som'sett gent.=

William=   John   =   Elizabeth da.=William Walton 3=Joane da. of —
Walton   Walton   of — Longe.   sonne of Shop-   Lee of the Isle
1 sonne.   2 sonne.   wike.   of Wight.

Richard   Thomas   Alex-   Henry Wal-   Richard Wal-   Dunstan Wal-=Blanch
Walton   Walton. ander   ton 3 sonne. ton eldest   ton, 2 sonne da. of
his   —   sonne.   citizen &   Will'm
only   An-   Robt 4   —   mercer of   Wat-
sonne.   drew.   sonne.   Jane married   London.   son of
                            —   to Geffry   Lon-
                            Francis 5   Shercome.   don.
                            sonne.

Wilkynson.

ARMS. *Quarterly :—1 and 4. Gules, a fess vair between two unicorns courant or. 2. Ermine, on a chevron engrailed sable three roses argent.* (GILBERD.) *3. Argent, a fess gules between three parrots vert beaked and collared of the second.* (LOMLEY.)

John Wilkynson of Gold- =Jane da. and heyre of John Gilberd sonne & heire of
hanger in com. Essex   Nicholas Gilberd and Elizabeth his wife da. and
gent.   heyre of Will'm Lomley 3 sonne to Rafe Lomley
                          first Lo. Lomley.

Gilbert Wilkynson 1 sonne=Anne da. of — Glynne.   Christopher Wilkynson 2
of Goldhanger.   sonne.

Richard Wilkynson 1=Agnes da.   John 2   Olive maried to   Mary maried to
sonne Citizen and   of Amp-   sonne.   Nicholas Grave.   John Davy of
Draper of London.   cotts.   Essex.

Thomas Wilkinson   2. John.   3. Peter.   4 Christopher.   Martha 1 da.
1 sonne.

Dawbney.

ARMS. *Gules, five fusils conjoined in fess argent, on the centre one a fleur-de-lis sable.*

John Dawbney of London, gent.═Alice da. of — Edes of Warwickshier.

Oliver Dawbney of ═Elizabeth da. of
London, gent.   — Drayner.

Joane maried to — Higgins of London.

Rowland Dawbney.

Anne.

Dove.

ARMS. *Sable, a fess dancetté ermine between three doves argent, beaked and legged gules; in chief a crescent or for difference.*
CREST. *A dove argent, wings sable, charged with a crescent for difference.*

Henry Dove of Stradbroke in com. Suff. gent.═Alice da. of — Nowell.

Christopher Dove, eldest sonne.

Robert Dove 2═Lettice da. of
sonne Citizen   Nicholas
and March[t]   Bull of Lon-
Taylor of   don.
London.

Joane maried to Nicholas H.

Eleonor maried to Nicholas Harison of London.

Robert Dove 1 sonne.   2. John.   3. Henry.   4 Thomas.   5 Richard.

Astry.

ARMS. *Barry wavy of six argent and azure, on a chief gules three bezants; a crescent for difference.*

S[r] Rafe Astrey, Knight, he maried to his 1 wife,═Margarett da. of — Hill.
Margery by whom he had no issue.

William Astry 1 sonne═Isabell da. of — Pigott of Bechington
and heyre.   in com. Buck.

Rafe Astry 2 sonne.

Thomas Astry 1 sonne.

Francis Astry 2═Elizabeth da. of Oliver
sonne of Lon- Smyth of London.
don, gent.

Elizabeth maried to William Bugby of Huntingdonshire.

Sowdeak.

ARMS. *Argent, on a fess dancetté gules an annulet or, from the sinister chief an arm issuing from clouds proper vested gules, touching in the chief point a heart of the last between two spear-heads sable, pointing inwards.*

CREST. *A dexter arm erect, couped at the elbow, vested gules, charged with an annulet or, cuffed with a frill argent, holding in the hand proper a heart of the first.*

William Sowdeak al's Sowtheak of Comberland.=Isabell da. of — Hutton.

| John Sudeke 1 sonne. | Thomas 2 sonne. — William 3 sonne. | George Sowdeake 5 sonne, citizen and grocer of London. | =Elizabeth da. of Philip Gonter of London. | Anthony 4 sonne. |

William Soudeak.   Anne.

Heton.

ARMS. *Quarterly:—1 and 4. Argent, on a bend engrailed sable three bulls' heads couped of the field. 2 and 3. Argent, a Moor's head sable banded round the forehead of the first and second, between three fleurs-de-lis of the second.*

CREST. *Out of a ducal coronet gules, a bull's head argent.*

Bryan Heton of Lancashier.=Catarine da. of Thurston Anderton of Anderton.

| William Heton 1 sonne, Citizen & Marchant Taylor of London. | =Rose da. of John Copwood of Tatredge in com. Hertf. ARMS. *Argent, from the dexter chief a pile engrailed gules, surmounted by another sable between two eagles displayed vert.* | James Heton 2 sonne. | Augustyne 3 sonne. | 4 Albany Heton. |

Awdrey.   Anne.

Barney.

ARMS. *Per pale azure and gules, a cross engrailed argent.*

John Barney of Reedham in=Margaret da. of Sir Roger Wentworth Norff.   of Coddam in Essex.

| John Barney 1 sonne. | Robert Barney=Margarett da. of — 2 sonne of Kenrick widow of London gent. Edmond Garway of London. | Mary 1 da. maried to Robert Jenney after to — Brampton. | Amy 2 daughter. |

Anne his only daughter.

Sanforde.

ARMS. *Argent, on a chevron between three doves sable, beaked and legged gules, an annulet or.*

Hugh Sanforde of Miluerton in com. Somersetsh. gent.=Maud his wife.

William Sanforde.=Agnes da. of Nicolas Rodway.

John Sanforde=Agnes da. of — Bonvile.

Anne da. of . . .=John Sanforde of Mil-=Margarett da. of Andrew Harlewyn
       uerton.   of Colompton.

Richard Sanforde.	James. — Alice.	Bartholomew 1 sonne. — Xpofer 2 sonne unto whome the land was conveyed.	3. George. — 4 Henry.	Edward Sanforde 5 sonne Citizen & Marchantaylor of London.	=Marg'y da. of Giles Bruges of London Draper.	Baldwyn Sanforde 6 sonne.

Benne.

ARMS. *Argent, a fess dancetté gules between three dragons' heads erased vert.*
CREST. *A tiger statant ermine, ducally gorged and tufted or.*

Henry Benne of Saffron Walden in Essex.=

John Benne, yeoman of the Crowne=— da. of John Burrell of Wormley in
to King H. 7 and H. 8.   com. Hertf. Sergeant at Armes to K. H.
            7 and H. 8.

Thomas Benne 1 sonne ob. s. p.	Robert Benne=Elizabeth da. and coheyre Citizen and of Reignold Woodeson. Ironmonger ARMS. *Or, on a cross azure,* of London. *pierced of the field, four* *eagles displayed or.*	Mercy first maried to . . . Robson after to . . . Derick.

Anthony Benne.   John Benne.

Longe.

ARMS. *Sable semé of crosses crosslet, a lion rampant argent within a bordure engrailed or.*

Simon Longe of London, gent.=Alice da. of — Huglett who maried the da. of — Kirkby of Essex.

Morris Longe Citizen & Clothworker of=Margaret da. of — Hamond of Hartfordshire his 1 wife. — London he maried to his 2nd wife Jane da. of — Mayte of Abingdon.

Mary maried to Wm Allen of London Alderman.

| John Longe 1 sonne. | 2. Anthony. — 3. Willm. — 4. Robt. | 5. George. — 6. Morris. — 7. Simon. | Alice. — Mary. — Anne. | Margaret. | Elizab. | Juditha. |

Lason.

ARMS. *Per pale argent and sable, a chevron counterchanged, in chief an annulet or.*
CREST. *Out of clouds proper two arms embowed vested ermine, holding in the hands proper a sun in splendour or.*

William Lason of Osworth in the=— da. of John Hedworth of Harverton. — Bishoprick of Durham.

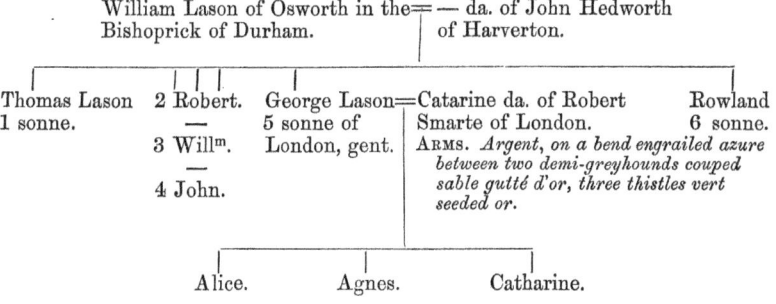

| Thomas Lason 1 sonne. | 2 Robert. — 3 Willm. — 4 John. | George Lason 5 sonne of London, gent. | =Catarine da. of Robert Smarte of London. ARMS. *Argent, on a bend engrailed azure between two demi-greyhounds couped sable gutté d'or, three thistles vert seeded or.* | Rowland 6 sonne. |

| Alice. | Agnes. | Catharine. |

Okeover.

ARMS. *Ermine, on a chief gules three bezants, the centre one charged with a mullet sable.*
CREST. *An oak-tree vert, acorned or.*

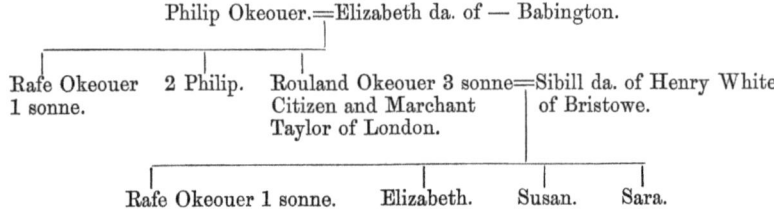

Philip Okeouer.═Elizabeth da. of — Babington.

Rafe Okeouer 1 sonne.   2 Philip.   Rouland Okeouer 3 sonne═Sibill da. of Henry White Citizen and Marchant Taylor of London. of Bristowe.

Rafe Okeouer 1 sonne.   Elizabeth.   Susan.   Sara.

Wanton.

ARMS. *Quarterly :—1 and 4. Argent, a chevron and in dexter chief an annulet sable.*
2. Ermine, a chevron engrailed between three griffins' heads erased gules.
(LAXTON.) *3. Ermine, a chief indented gules.*
CREST. *An eagle preying on a dove proper.*

Thomas Wanton citizen and═Joane da. of John Laxton and heyre to Sr Wm Grocer of London. Laxton brother of the sayd John.

1 John Wanton═Mary da. of 1 sonne of Will'm London gent. Ramsey of London Grocer.   2 William. — 3 Thomas. — 4 Nicholas.   Catarine maried to William Bodnam of London, grocer.   Mary maried to Rob't Farrar.   Martha.

Browne.

ARMS. *Gules, a griffin segreant or, a chief indented per fess of the second and ermine.*
CREST. *A mountain-cat ermine.*

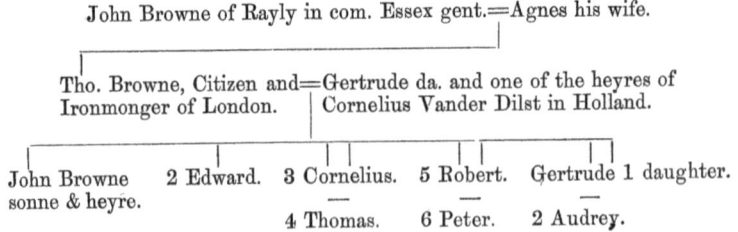

John Browne of Rayly in com. Essex gent.═Agnes his wife.

Tho. Browne, Citizen and═Gertrude da. and one of the heyres of Ironmonger of London. Cornelius Vander Dilst in Holland.

John Browne sonne & heyre.   2 Edward.   3 Cornelius. — 4 Thomas.   5 Robert. — 6 Peter.   Gertrude 1 daughter. — 2 Audrey.

𝔚𝔞𝔶𝔢𝔯.

ARMS. *Or, two lions passant in pale azure within a bordure gules charged with eight martlets or.*

| Bethsaba daughter of — Cortes. | = | Thomas Wayer of London gent, Citizen and Fishmonger of London. | = | — da. of — Bluett 1 wife. |

| Richard Wayer 2 sonne. | 3 Isack. — 4 Jacob. | Susan. — Anne. | Eliz. — Bethsaba. | | Thomas Wayre al's Wayere his eldest sonne. |

𝔓attenson.

ARMS. *Argent, on a fess sable three fleurs-de-lis or.*
CREST. *Out of a ducal coronet proper a horse's head sable semé of plates.*

| John Pattenson of Cheriburton in com. Ebor gent. | = | Ellen da. of Bryan Chew Knight. |

| Joh'nes Patenson 1 sonne. | Brianus Patenson Citizen and Vintonner of London 2 sonne. | = | Alice da. of William Kede of litle holme al's of the Wood in the County of York. |

| Brian Patenson 1 sonne. | 2 Robert. | Christian. | Prudence. |

𝔅ackhouse.

ARMS. *Per saltire azure and or, a saltire couped ermine.*
CREST. *An eagle vert, armed or, wings closed, preying upon a snake proper.*

| Thomas Backhouse of Whitrige in com. Cumbr. gent. | = | Elen da. of John Parkyn of Hartloo in Cumb'land. |

| Nicholas Backhowse gent. | = | Anne da. of Tho. Curson of Croxall in Darbishier. |
| | | ARMS. *Quarterly :—1 and 4. Azure, on a bend between two lions rampant argent, three popinjays vert, beaked and legged gules. 2. Vairy or and gules, on a chief sable, three horseshoes argent. 3. Gules, on a bend argent three martlets sable.* |

| Samuel Backhouse 1 sonne. | 2. Miles. — 3. Rowland. | Sara maried to Nicholas Fuller Counsellor at lawe, alias Fulwer. | Mary. |

𝔚arner.

ARMS. *Quarterly:*—1 *and* 4. *Or, a chevron between three boars' heads couped sable.*
2. *Or, a fess dancetté sable, in chief a martlet gules.* (VAVASOR.) 3. *Per pale or and argent, three crescents ermines.*
CREST. *A horse's head erased per fess ermine and gules.*

John Warner of London Alderman.═

John Warner of Haring═Elizabeth da. of Vavasor and brother to
in com. Midd. Ar. | Justice Vavasor of Yorkshier.

| William Warner s. p. | Robert Warner 2 sonne of Strowd in com. Midd. brother & heyre to William. | ═Julian da. and heyre of John Greene of London brother & heyre of Sergeant Greene. | Elizabeth maried to William Bearde of Midd. gent. |

Anne da. and coheyre═Marke Warner Esqʳ of London and═Elizabeth da. of
of William Robyns of | Midd. sonne & heyre. | Philip Meredith of
London, Alderman. | His 3ᵈ wife was Thomasin da. of | London gent. 2
  | William Browne of Flamberds in | wife.
  | Essex. |

| Elizabeth maried to Tho. Stamp of Avenon in com. Bark. gent. | John Warner sonne & heyre. | Other sonnes without issue. |

They are dwelling at Strowte Greene in Midlesex.

Offley.

ARMS. *Argent, on a cross flory azure between four Cornish choughs sable, beaked and legs gules, a lion passant guardant or.*
CREST. *A demi-lion rampant per pale or and azure, collar counterchanged, holding in his paws an olive branch vert fructed or.*

Offley duxit filiam — Cradoke.═

Sʳ Thomas Offley obijt die═Joane da. of John Nichells and his sole heyre.
Mercurij, 29 Augᵗ 1582 | ARMS. *Quarterly:*—1 *and* 4. *Azure, on a chevron or*
inter horas 2 & 3 in | *between two eagles displayed in chief, and in base a lion*
matutino. | *passant of the last, a hurt charged with a leopard's head*
  | *argent, enclosed by two torteaux, each charged with an*
  | *escallop of the third.* 2 *and* 3. *Argent, a chevron gules*
  | *between four tassels sable.*

Henry Offley his only sonne and heyre.═Mary da. to Sir John White Knight.

Thomas.

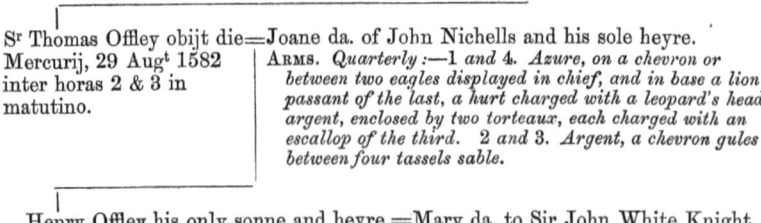

Anes.

ARMS. *Argent, a lion rampant guardant gules within an orle of torteaux.*

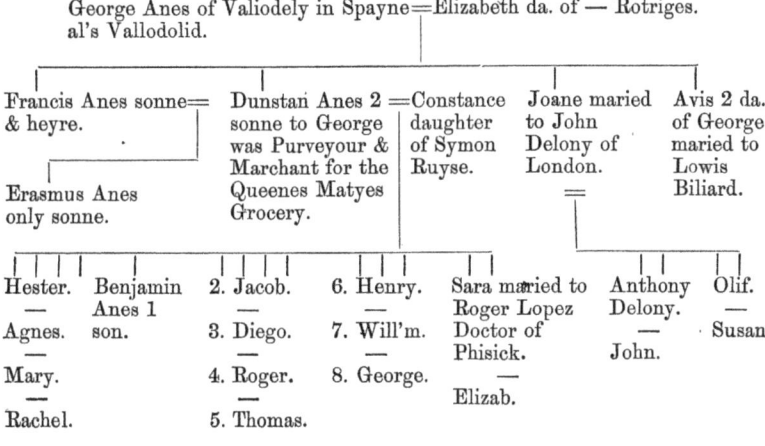

George Anes of Valiodely in Spayne=Elizabeth da. of — Rotriges.
al's Vallodolid.

Francis Anes sonne= Dunstan Anes 2 =Constance   Joane maried   Avis 2 da.
& heyre.   sonne to George   daughter   to John   of George
                      was Purveyour &   of Symon   Delony of   maried to
                      Marchant for the Ruyse.   London.   Lowis
Erasmus Anes   Queenes Matyes   Biliard.
only sonne.   Grocery.

Hester.   Benjamin   2. Jacob.   6. Henry.   Sara maried to   Anthony   Olif.
—   Anes 1   —   —   Roger Lopez   Delony.   —
Agnes.   son.   3. Diego.   7. Will'm. Doctor of   —   Susan.
—   —   —   Phisick.   John.
Mary.   4. Roger.   8. George. —
—   —   Elizab.
Rachel.   5. Thomas.

Bradbery.

ARMS. *Quarterly:—1 and 4. Sable, a chevron ermine between three round buckles
argent. 2 and 3. Argent, a chevron between three chess rooks sable.*
CREST. *A demi-dove argent, fretty gules, holding in the beak a slip of barberry vert,
fructed of the first.*

John Bradbury of Lichfield Gent.=Elizabeth da. of — Leftchilde.

John Bradbery 1   John Bradbery 2=Joane da. of Thomas Wison of
sonne.   sonne.   Bednoll grene.

Thomas Bradbery   John 2 sonne.   3 Jonas.   4 Richard.   6 Peter.   Eliz.
1 sonne.   —
                                              5 Edward.   Helen.

Rigges.

ARMS. *Gules, a fess between three water-spaniels argent, each holding in their
mouths a bird bolt in bend or.*
CREST. *A water-spaniel argent, holding in its mouth a bird bolt or.*

Cooper.

ARMS. *Argent, three martlets gules, on a chief engrailed of the second as many annulets or.*
CREST. *A lion's gamb erect or, holding a branch vert, fructed gules.*

Richard Cooper of Madeley in com. Salop.=

Editha da. of — Smith=Richard Cooper=Sibill da. of William Hopkyns of
of London.　　　　　　of London gent.　Hanbery in Worcestershire.

Lionell Cooper his sonne & heyre.

Philipson.

ARMS. *Sable, a chevron ermine between three bats expanded argent.*
CREST. *A horse's head or, crined sable, holding in his mouth an oak branch vert, acorned or.*

Mathew Philipson of Kendall in com.=Anne da. of — Boothe of
Ebor gent.　　　　　　　　　　　　Lincolnshier.

Robert Philipson=Margaret da. of John　Mark 2　Elizabeth maried to John
sonne & heyre of　Parker of London.　sonne.　Coxston of London.
London, gent.　ARMS. *Argent, on a fess*
　　　　　　between three pheons sable, as many bezants.

Nicolls.

ARMS. *Azure, a fess between three lions' heads erased or.*
CREST. *A tiger sejant ermine.*

Christian da. of=John Nicolls of London, gent at this=Ellen da. of James Holt
— Thomson 1　present controller of the workes at　of Stubley in Com. Lanc.
wife.　　　　London Bridge and all other lands　ARMS. *Argent, on a bend*
　　　　　　and revenues of the same, & in　*engrailed sable, three*
　　　　　　charge for provision of Corne for　*fleurs-de-lis of the field.*
　　　　　　the City of London.

Mary maried to Francis　Elizabeth maried to Edmond Cook of Lizenes
Garrad.　　　　　　　in Kent, gent.

Sares.

ARMS. *Gules, a chevron argent between three Saracens' heads couped at the shoulders or, eyes proper.*

CREST. *A goat's head erased argent, armed or.*

Humfrey Sares of Title in com. Ebor gent.=

Edmond Sares of Horsham in=Joane da. of — Day of Title
Sussex gent.   in Yorkshier.

| John Sares of Sandwich 1 sonne. | Catarine da. of Edw. Lovell. ARMS. *Argent, a chevron between three wolves' heads erased gules.* | =Thomas Sares *alias* Saris of London gent. | =Catarine da. of Henr. Chevall of London Draper. ARMS *Or, three nags' heads couped sable, bridled argent.* | Joane maried to Edmond Lane of London. |

| John Sares 1 sonne. | 2 Henry. | Joane maried to Richard Bushe of London. | Richard Sares. | George. |

Grange.

ARMS. *Azure, a chevron between three lions rampant or, on a chief of the second three escallops gules within a bordure compony of the second and last.*

CREST. *A griffin's head erased sable, beaked and eared or, charged with three bezants.*

Richard Grange.=

John Grange of Wolsingham in com. Cestr.=Alice his wife.

George Grange sonne and heyre of Bishops=Margaret da. of Rob't Johnson of
Aukland in com. Dunelm.   Hunwike in com. Dunelm.

John Grange Citizen and Haberdasher of=Elizabeth da. of Thomas Dow-
London sonne & heyre.   thwayte of Cumberland.

John Grange sonne   Susan maried to Robert Davis of
& heyre.   High Holborne gent.

Ramsey.

ARMS. *Sable, a chevron ermine between three rams' heads erased argent, horned or.*
CREST. *A griffin's head erased per fess indented argent and sable, in base guttée d'or.*

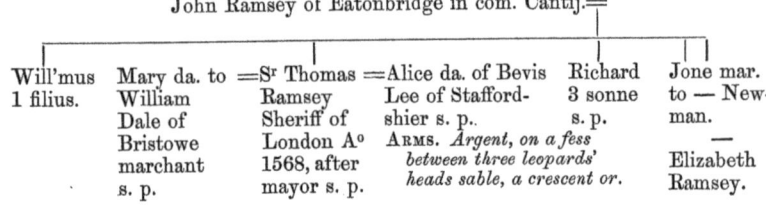

John Ramsey of Eatonbridge in com. Cantij.=

| Will'mus 1 filius. | Mary da. to William Dale of Bristowe marchant s. p. | =Sʳ Thomas Ramsey Sheriff of London Aº 1568, after mayor s. p. | =Alice da. of Bevis Lee of Staffordshier s. p.. ARMS. *Argent, on a fess between three leopards' heads sable, a crescent or.* | Richard 3 sonne s. p. | Jone mar. to — Newman. — Elizabeth Ramsey. |

Birde.

ARMS. *Quarterly :—1 and 4. Per pale or and argent, an eagle displayed sable. 2 and 3. Quarterly gules and or, in the first and fourth three fleurs-de-lis argent, over all a trefoil slipped azure.* (MASSIE.)
CREST. *A griffin's head erased bendy of six sable and argent.*

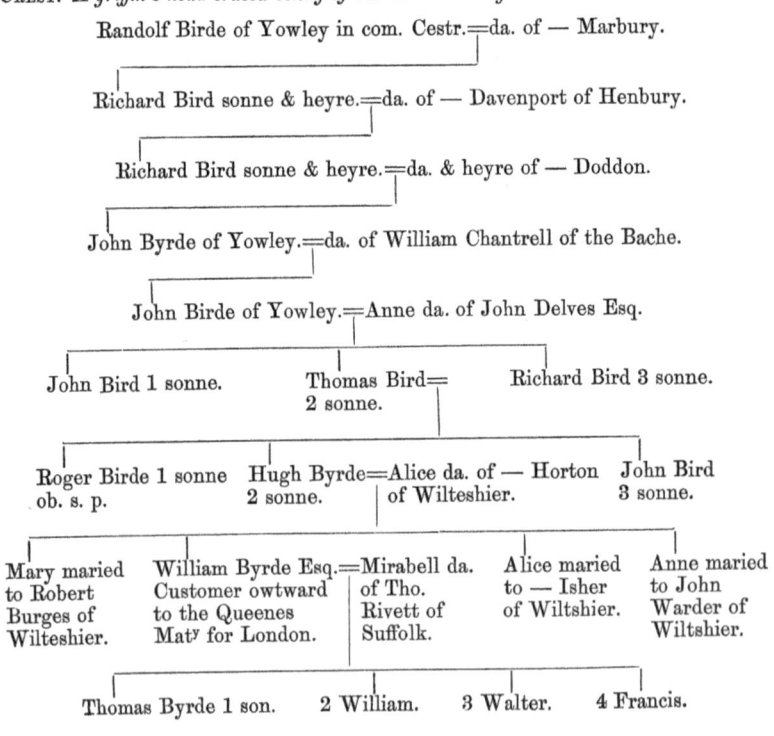

Randolf Birde of Yowley in com. Cestr.=da. of — Marbury.

Richard Bird sonne & heyre.=da. of — Davenport of Henbury.

Richard Bird sonne & heyre.=da. & heyre of — Doddon.

John Byrde of Yowley.=da. of William Chantrell of the Bache.

John Birde of Yowley.=Anne da. of John Delves Esq.

| John Bird 1 sonne. | Thomas Bird= 2 sonne. | Richard Bird 3 sonne. |

| Roger Birde 1 sonne ob. s. p. | Hugh Byrde= 2 sonne. | =Alice da. of — Horton of Wilteshier. | John Bird 3 sonne. |

| Mary maried to Robert Burges of Wilteshier. | William Byrde Esq.= Customer owtward to the Queenes Matʸ for London. | =Mirabell da. of Tho. Rivett of Suffolk. | Alice maried to — Isher of Wiltshier. | Anne maried to John Warder of Wiltshier. |

| Thomas Byrde 1 son. | 2 William. | 3 Walter. | 4 Francis. |

𝕾myth.

ARMS. *Per pale or and azure, a chevron argent between three lions counterchanged.*
CREST. *A tiger's head erased argent pelletté, collared sable bezanté and chained or.*

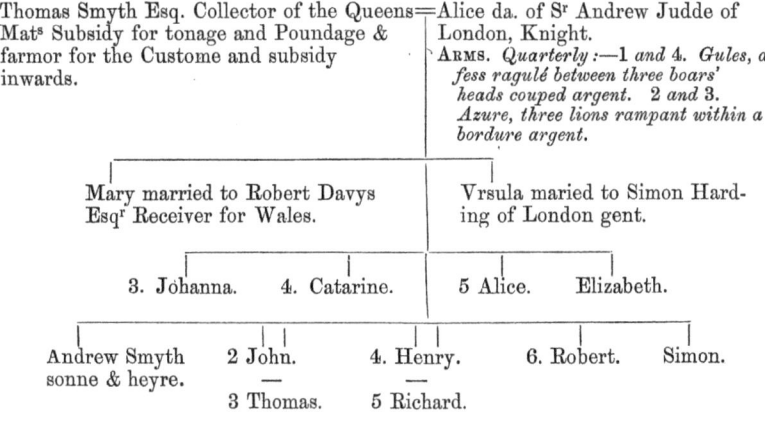

Thomas Smyth Esq. Collector of the Queens=Alice da. of Sr Andrew Judde of
Mats Subsidy for tonage and Poundage & London, Knight.
farmor for the Custome and subsidy ARMS. *Quarterly :—1 and 4. Gules, a*
inwards. *fess ragulé between three boars'*
heads couped argent. 2 and 3.
Azure, three lions rampant within a
bordure argent.

Mary married to Robert Davys
Esqr Receiver for Wales.

Vrsula maried to Simon Harding of London gent.

3. Johanna. 4. Catarine.

5 Alice. Elizabeth.

Andrew Smyth
sonne & heyre.

2 John.

3 Thomas.

4. Henry.

5 Richard.

6. Robert. Simon.

Billingsley.

ARMS. *Argent, within a cross voided between four lions rampant five estoiles sable.*

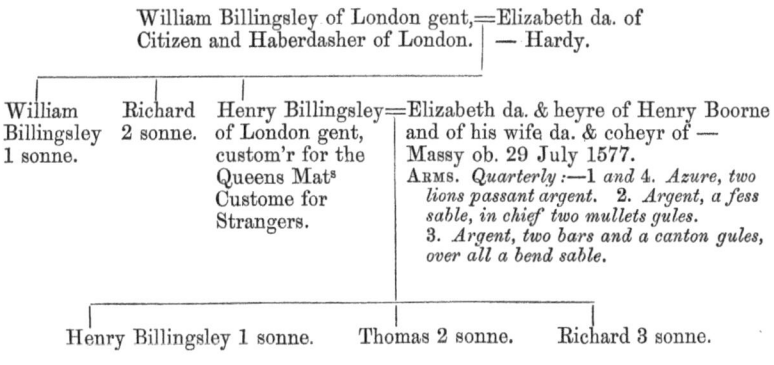

William Billingsley of London gent,=Elizabeth da. of
Citizen and Haberdasher of London. — Hardy.

William
Billingsley
1 sonne.

Richard
2 sonne.

Henry Billingsley=Elizabeth da. & heyre of Henry Boorne
of London gent, and of his wife da. & coheyr of —
custom'r for the Massy ob. 29 July 1577.
Queens Mats ARMS. *Quarterly :—1 and 4. Azure, two*
Custome for *lions passant argent. 2. Argent, a fess*
Strangers. *sable, in chief two mullets gules.*
3. Argent, two bars and a canton gules,
over all a bend sable.

Henry Billingsley 1 sonne. Thomas 2 sonne. Richard 3 sonne.

Grey.

ARMS. *Barry of six argent and azure, on a bend gules a rose of the field.*
CREST. *On a mount vert a bear argent.*

Richard Grey gent. descended of a younger brother of — Grey of Rotherfeild.

Walter Grey his son and heir.

Margery da. of — Henley of Cornwall. = Richard Grey of London, gent. Searcher for the Queenes Mat^yes Custome. = Dorothy da. of Simon Lynch of Cranbrok in Kent.
ARMS. *Sable, three leopards rampant argent, spotted of the field.*

Mathew Grey 4 sonne.   Humfrey 5.   Helena.   William Grey sonne and heyre.   2 Henry. — 3 Edmond.   Margarett maried to Willm Langhorne of London, drap.

Young.

James Young of Charnes in com. Staff. = Anne da. of — Perivs of Shropshier.

John Young 1 sonne.   Richard Yonng of London. Packer to the Strangers. = Joane da. of — Croston of Westchester.   3 Humfry.   Margery mar. to — Dickons of com. Bedf.   Dorothy mar. to — Manwaring of Pever Cheshier.   Anne maried to Roger Hinton of Richardon in Shropshier.

Francis Younge sonne & heyre.

Kayle *sive* Kele.

ARMS. *Quarterly embattled argent and sable, in first quarter a mullet counterchanged.*
CREST. *A wyvern argent, wings or.*

Philipps.

ARMS. *Or, a lion rampant sable, ducally gorged and chained of the field.*
CREST. *A lion sejant sable, ducally gorged and chained or.*

Robert Philipps of — =Elizabetha daughter of — Mampas.

John Philipps sonne and heyre.=Joane da. of Richard Clayton.

William Philipps of London gent.=Joane da. of Tho. Houghton.
one of the Queens Mat⁵ Cus-   ARMS. *Sable, three bars argent,*
tomers for the Wooll.   *in dexter chief a bezant.*

Lovell.

ARMS. *Argent, a chevron sable between three foxes' heads erased gules.*

Henry Lovell of Skelton in com. Ebor. gent.=Margarett daughter of — Gay
a second brother of the same howse.   of Leicestershier.

Thomas Lovell of London gent.=Margarett da. of — Pikering
one of the Queenes Ma^tys   of Hasellwood in Yorkshire.
Customers for Wooll.

Elizabeth 1 daughter.   Elizabeth 2 daughter.   Margaret.

Wycliff.

ARMS. *Or, three bars azure.*
CREST. *A dragon's head argent.*

Woore.

ARMS. *Gules, a bend argent fretty sable, between three griffins' heads erased or.*
CREST. *Out of a ducal coronet or, a demi-heraldic panther argent spotted vert, gules
and azure, holding in his paw a branch of laurel slipped vert fructed gules.*

Richard Woore of London.=

Thwaytes.

[ARMS. *Argent, a cross sable, fretty of the field, in the first quarter a fleur-de-lis gules.*
CREST. *A game-cock proper, beaked and wattled gules, charged on the breast with a fleur-de-lis of the last.*
Granted by Wm. Dethick and Wm. Camden, Clarenceux, 1597.]

Thomas Thwaytes of Yorkshier.=

William Thwaytes of Cheping Wickham in com. Buck.=

William Thwaytes Citizen and Alderman of London (1597).

Turfeet of London.

ARMS. *Argent, an orle sable within an orle of eight martlets gules.*
CREST. *On a ducal coronet argent a stag trippant proper.*

Jackman.

ARMS. *Per saltire argent and sable, in chief and in base an eagle displayed counter-changed.*
CREST. *A griffin's head erased sable, gutty or.*

Edward Jackman, Alderman=Ann da. of Humphrey Pakington.
and Sheriff of London A° | ARMS. *Quarterly:—1 and 4. Per chevron sable*
Dⁿⁱ 1564. | *and argent in chief three mullets or, in base as*
                           | *many garbs gules.* 2. *Argent, on a fess between*
                           | *six martlets gules three quatrefoils of the field.*
                           | (WASHBOURNE.) 3. *Argent, on a bend azure*
                           | *three martlets or.* (HARDING.)

John Jackman, eldest sonne & heyre,=Jane 2 da. of Richard Lambart,
of London, grocer.   Alderman of London.

Edward Jackman of Hacton in the Liberty=Margaret da. of Sʳ Edward Sulliard
of Haveringe in the County of Essex.   of Fleminges in com. Essex Kᵗ.

2. John Jackman.=Jane da. of Peter Bettes-   1 Edward.   Anne m. Robert
                 worth of Com. Sussex.   Poleby.

Villett *alias* Violet.

ARMS. *Argent, on a chevron gules three towers triple-towered of the field, on a canton azure a fleur-de-lis or.*
CREST. *A tiger's head erased ermine, ducally gorged and tufted or.*

Henry Villett alias Violett of London and now of Kent.

Quarles.

John Quarles Esqr, Citizen & Draper of London, died 12 day of November 1577.

Tedcastle.

ARMS. *Quarterly :—1 and 4. Argent, three pales sable, on a chief azure as many lions' heads erased or. 2 and 3. Argent, on a fess gules three crescents or between two cotices wavy sable ; impaling vert a chevron between three roses or, a chief indented ermine.* (MAY.)
concess. p' R. Cook Clarenceux, A° D'ni 1590.

John Tedcastle of London sup'stes 1590.=Elizabeth May his wife.

Harison.

ARMS. *Quarterly :—1 and 4. Gules, an eagle displayed and a chief or. 2 and 3. Sable, a chevron between three dexter hands fessways clenehed argent, erased gules.*
CREST. *A snake vert entwined round a broken column or.*

— Harison of London Citizen.= — his wife da. of —.
ARMS. *Argent, a chevron ermines between three martlets sable.*
(EDWARDES or JARVIS?).

L

Colston.

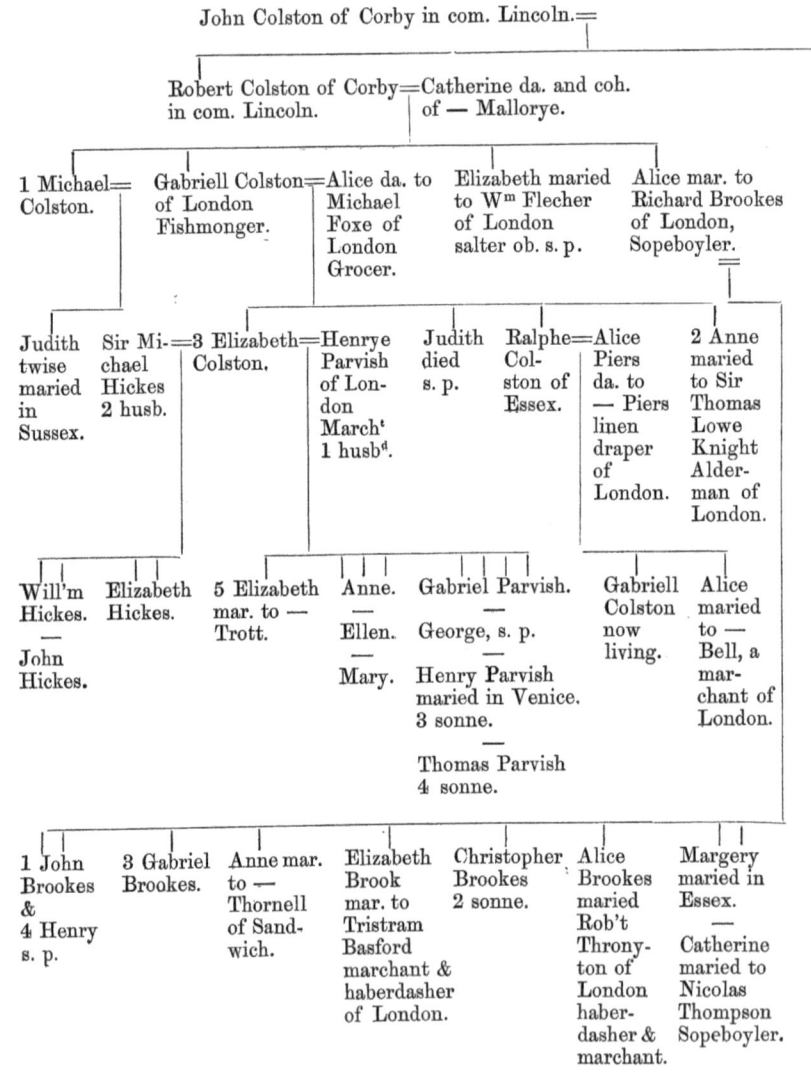

John Colston of Corby in com. Lincoln.═

Robert Colston of Corby═Catherine da. and coh.
in com. Lincoln. | of — Mallorye.

1 Michael═ | Gabriell Colston═Alice da. to | Elizabeth maried | Alice mar. to
Colston. | of London | Michael | to Wᵐ Flecher | Richard Brookes
  | Fishmonger. | Foxe of | of London | of London,
  | | London | salter ob. s. p. | Sopeboyler.
  | | Grocer. | | ═

Judith | Sir Mi-═3 Elizabeth═Henrye | Judith | Ralphe═Alice | 2 Anne
twise | chael | Colston. | Parvish | died | Col- | Piers | maried
maried | Hickes | | of Lon- | s. p. | ston of | da. to | to Sir
in | 2 husb. | | don | | Essex. | — Piers | Thomas
Sussex. | | | Marchᵗ | | | linen | Lowe
  | | | 1 husbᵈ. | | | draper | Knight
  | | | | | | of | Alder-
  | | | | | | London. | man of
  | | | | | | | London.

Will'm | Elizabeth | 5 Elizabeth | Anne. | Gabriel Parvish. | Gabriell | Alice
Hickes. | Hickes. | mar. to — | — | — | Colston | maried
— | | Trott. | Ellen. | George, s. p. | now | to —
John | | | — | — | living. | Bell, a
Hickes. | | | Mary. | Henry Parvish | | mar-
  | | | | maried in Venice. | | chant of
  | | | | 3 sonne. | | London.
			—	
			Thomas Parvish	
			4 sonne.	

1 John | 3 Gabriel | Anne mar. | Elizabeth | Christopher | Alice | Margery
Brookes | Brookes. | to — | Brook | Brookes | Brookes | maried in
& | | Thornell | mar. to | 2 sonne. | maried | Essex.
4 Henry | | of Sand- | Tristram | | Rob't | —
s. p. | | wich. | Basford | | Throny- | Catherine
  | | | marchant & | | ton of | maried to
  | | | haberdasher | | London | Nicolas
  | | | of London. | | haber- | Thompson
  | | | | | dasher & | Sopeboyler.
  | | | | | marchant. |

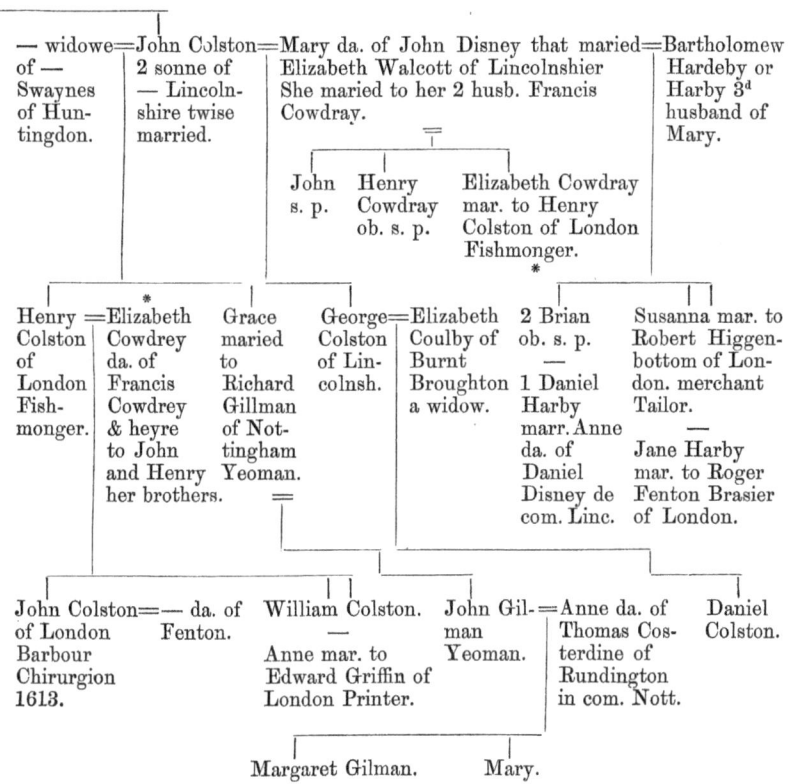

— widowe=John Colston=Mary da. of John Disney that maried=Bartholomew
of —   2 sonne of   Elizabeth Walcott of Lincolnshier   Hardeby or
Swaynes   — Lincoln-   She maried to her 2 husb. Francis   Harby 3ᵈ
of Hun-   shire twise   Cowdray.   husband of
tingdon.   married.   Mary.

John   Henry   Elizabeth Cowdray
s. p.   Cowdray   mar. to Henry
    ob. s. p.   Colston of London
    Fishmonger.

Henry =Elizabeth   Grace   George=Elizabeth   2 Brian   Susanna mar. to
Colston   Cowdrey   maried   Colston   Coulby of   ob. s. p.   Robert Higgen-
of   da. of   to   of Lin-   Burnt   —   bottom of Lon-
London   Francis   Richard   colnsh.   Broughton   1 Daniel   don. merchant
Fish-   Cowdrey   Gillman   a widow.   Harby   Tailor.
monger.   & heyre   of Not-   marr.Anne   —
    to John   tingham   da. of   Jane Harby
    and Henry   Yeoman.   Daniel   mar. to Roger
    her brothers.   Disney de   Fenton Brasier
    com. Linc.   of London.

John Colston=— da. of   William Colston.   John Gil-=Anne da. of   Daniel
of London   Fenton.   man   Thomas Cos-   Colston.
Barbour   Anne mar. to   Yeoman.   terdine of
Chirurgion   Edward Griffin of   Rundington
1613.   London Printer.   in com. Nott.

Margaret Gilman.   Mary.

𝔉𝔦𝔣𝔢𝔦𝔩𝔡 *alias* 𝔏𝔬𝔴𝔢.

ARMS. *Quarterly :—1 and 4. Per fess vert and argent a pale counterchanged, on the first three acorns or.* (FIFIELD.) *2 and 3. Argent, six ogresses, three, two, and one, a mullet gules.* (LACY.)

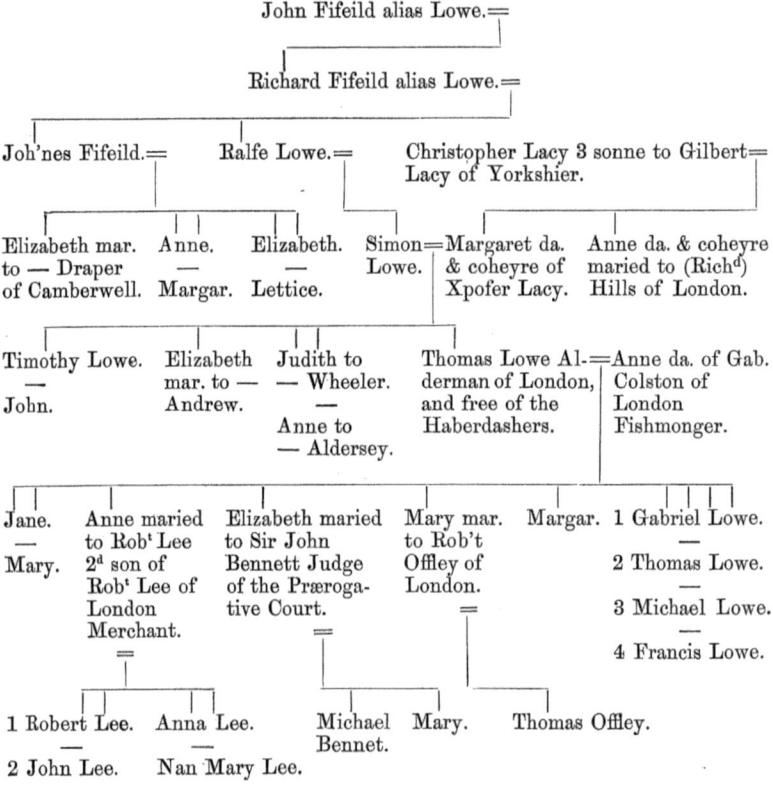

John Fifeild alias Lowe.=

Richard Fifeild alias Lowe.=

Joh'nes Fifeild.= Ralfe Lowe.= Christopher Lacy 3 sonne to Gilbert= Lacy of Yorkshier.

Elizabeth mar. to — Draper of Camberwell.　Anne. — Margar.　Elizabeth. — Lettice.　Simon= Lowe.　Margaret da. & coheyre of Xpofer Lacy.　Anne da. & coheyre maried to (Rich^d) Hills of London.

Timothy Lowe. — John.　Elizabeth mar. to — Andrew.　Judith to — Wheeler. — Anne to — Aldersey.　Thomas Lowe Al-= derman of London, and free of the Haberdashers.　Anne da. of Gab. Colston of London Fishmonger.

Jane. — Mary.　Anne maried to Robt Lee 2^d son of Robt Lee of London Merchant. =　Elizabeth maried to Sir John Bennett Judge of the Præroga- tive Court. =　Mary mar. to Rob't Offley of London. =　Margar.　1 Gabriel Lowe. — 2 Thomas Lowe. — 3 Michael Lowe. — 4 Francis Lowe.

1 Robert Lee. — 2 John Lee.　Anna Lee. — Nan Mary Lee.　Michael Bennet.　Mary.　Thomas Offley.

Sutton.

ARMS. *Or, a lion rampant vert, a canton ermine.*
CREST. *A demi-lion rampant vert.*

William Sutton sonne of — Sutton of Ediall in com. Staffordiæ.⹀

John Sutton of Henley sup' Thames=Elizabeth da. of — Tailor of
in com. Oxon.   Ediall in com. Staff.

Richard Sutton of London Esquier=Elizabeth da. of George Fishe
now Auditor. 1612.   of Ayott Montfichett.

— filia et hæres nupta Jacobo Altham milit. filio Baronis de S'c'cio.

Shaa.

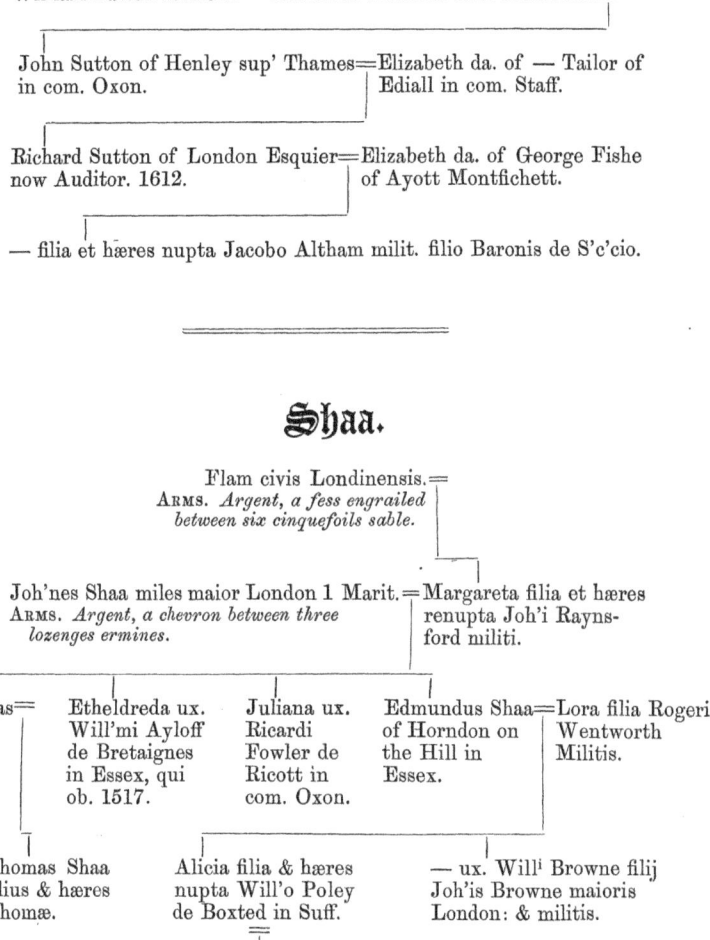

Flam civis Londinensis.⹀
ARMS. *Argent, a fess engrailed
between six cinquefoils sable.*

Joh'nes Shaa miles maior London 1 Marit.=Margareta filia et hæres
ARMS. *Argent, a chevron between three   renupta Joh'i Rayns-
lozenges ermines.*   ford militi.

Thomas=   Etheldreda ux.   Juliana ux.   Edmundus Shaa=Lora filia Rogeri
Shaa.   Will'mi Ayloff   Ricardi   of Horndon on   Wentworth
            de Bretaignes   Fowler de   the Hill in   Militis.
            in Essex, qui   Ricott in   Essex.
            ob. 1517.   com. Oxon.

Thomas Shaa   Alicia filia & hæres   — ux. Will[i] Browne filij
filius & hæres   nupta Will'o Poley   Joh'is Browne maioris
Thomæ.   de Boxted in Suff.   London: & militis.

Johannes Poley de Boxted.

Haydon.

ARMS. *Quarterly of six :*—1. *Argent, three bars gemelles azure, on a chief gules a bar dancetté or.* (HAYDON.) 2. *Ermine, three battle-axes (sable), in chief a crescent.* (WEEKES.) 3. *Argent, two chevrons within a bordure engrailed gules.* (KYMBER.) 4. *Ermine, two surgeons' flams in saltire gules.* (TIDERLEIGH.) 5. *Argent, two chevrons azure within a bordure engrailed gules, a martlet (sable) for difference.* 6. *Argent, ten torteaux, four, three, two, and one, a label of three points azure.* (BABINGTON.)

CREST. *A lion argent, seizing on a bull courant sable.*

MOTTO. *" Ferme en foy."*

Joh'nes de Haydon.=

Robertus de Haydon de Bonghwood 19 Edw. 1.=Joane the wife of Robert.

Henry Hay-=Juliana   Roger Heydon de   Peter Haydon brother   Merand
don 19 E.   uxor   Nether Stowford   and heyre of Roger 7 E. 1.   sister of
1.   ejus.   7 E. 1.   Peeter

William Haydon=   Johannes Hay-   Adam Haydon filius naturalis.
sonne & heyre   don died of the ARMS. *Argent, three bars gemelles azure, on*
of Henry.   Plague.   *a chief gules a bar dancetté or, within a*
                                    bordure compony of the third and fourth.

John Heydon.   Henry Heydon of Bowood & Epforde Aº 20 R. 2.=

John Haydon of Bowood & Epforde Aº 8 H. 4.=

Richard Haydon of Bowood & Epforde 15=   Henry Kelly=Eliz. da. & heyre
E. 4.   of Kelly.   of Kymber.

Agnes da. — Merifeeld=Richard Heydon=Joane da.   Richard=Alice =Richard
2 wife.   of Bowod and   of Morice   Weekes Kelley Cople-
ARMS. *Argent, a chevron* Epforde 13 H. 8. Trent 1 1 hus-   da. of ston 2
gules between three   wife.   band.   Henry. husbᵈ.
falcons rising proper.

George Haydon   Joh'nes Hay-   Joane wife of   Thomas=Joane   Isota nupta
of Hornsayes, 3 don of Cadhey, John Corham.   Hay-   da. &   Ric'o Wood.
sonne mar.   2 filius married ARMS. *Argent,* don of heyre
Susan da. of —   Joane da. of   *a cross sable* Bowod   of   Christoferus
Park of Lon-   Robert Gren-   *between four*   & Ep-   Rich-   Wood duxit
don.   vill.   *eagles dis-*   forde 1 ard   filiam Joh'is
ARMS. *Sable, on a*   *played gules.*   sonne. Weekes. Wyndham
fess engrailed argent between three   militis.
hinds trippant or as many tor-
teaux, each charged with a pheon
of the second.

A   B

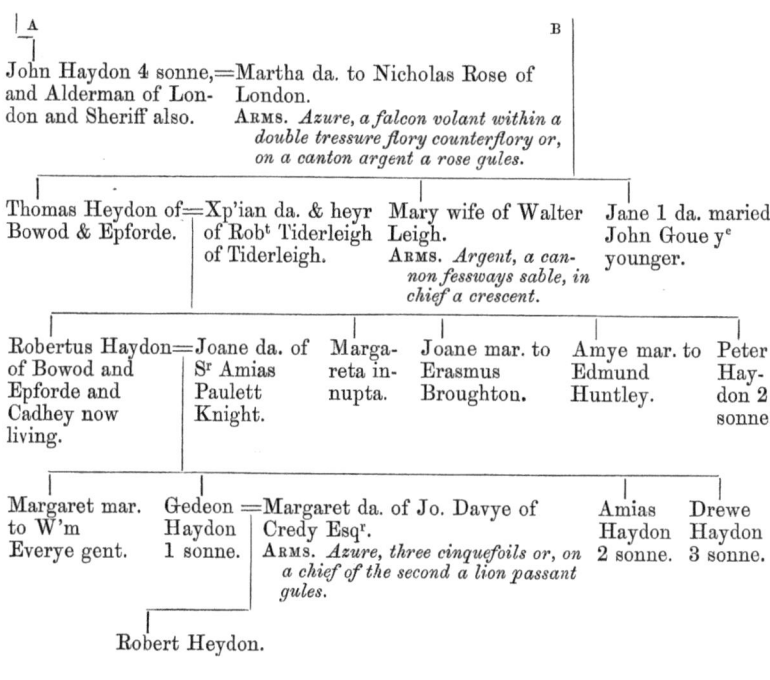

| A | | B |

John Haydon 4 sonne,=Martha da. to Nicholas Rose of
and Alderman of Lon- London.
don and Sheriff also. ARMS. *Azure, a falcon volant within a*
double tressure flory counterflory or,
on a canton argent a rose gules.

Thomas Heydon of=Xp'ian da. & heyr Mary wife of Walter Jane 1 da. maried
Bowod & Epforde. of Robt Tiderleigh Leigh. John Goue ye
of Tiderleigh. ARMS. *Argent, a can-* younger.
non fessways sable, in
chief a crescent.

Robertus Haydon=Joane da. of Marga- Joane mar. to Amye mar. to Peter
of Bowod and Sr Amias reta in- Erasmus Edmund Hay-
Epforde and Paulett nupta. Broughton. Huntley. don 2
Cadhey now Knight. sonne.
living.

Margaret mar. Gedeon =Margaret da. of Jo. Davye of Amias Drewe
to W'm Haydon Credy Esqr. Haydon Haydon
Everye gent. 1 sonne. ARMS. *Azure, three cinquefoils or, on* 2 sonne. 3 sonne.
a chief of the second a lion passant
gules.

Robert Heydon.

Bruges.

ARMS. *Argent, on a cross sable a leopard's head, and in chief a crescent or.*

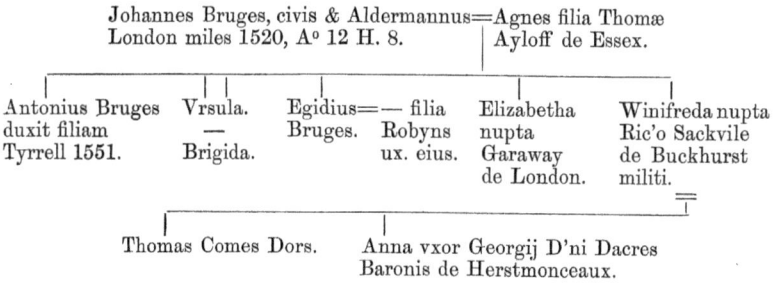

Johannes Bruges, civis & Aldermannus=Agnes filia Thomæ
London miles 1520, Aº 12 H. 8. Ayloff de Essex.

Antonius Bruges Vrsula. Egidius=— filia Elizabetha Winifreda nupta
duxit filiam — Bruges. Robyns nupta Ric'o Sackvile
Tyrrell 1551. Brigida. ux. eius. Garaway de Buckhurst
de London. militi.

Thomas Comes Dors. Anna vxor Georgij D'ni Dacres
Baronis de Herstmonceaux.

Peacock.

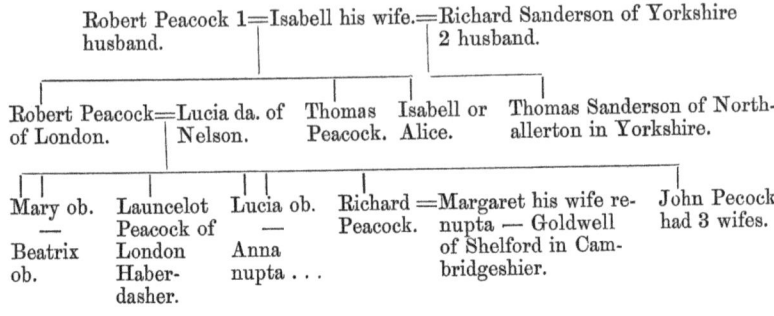

Robert Peacock 1=Isabell his wife.=Richard Sanderson of Yorkshire
husband.   2 husband.

Robert Peacock=Lucia da. of   Thomas   Isabell or   Thomas Sanderson of North-
of London. | Nelson.   Peacock.   Alice.   allerton in Yorkshire.

Mary ob.   Launcelot   Lucia ob.   Richard =Margaret his wife re-   John Pecock
—   Peacock of   —   Peacock. nupta — Goldwell   had 3 wifes.
Beatrix   London   Anna   of Shelford in Cam-
ob.   Haber-   nupta . . .   bridgeshier.
            dasher.

Sotherton.

ARMS. *Argent, a fess and in chief two crescents gules.*

Thomas Sotherton of Ludham.=

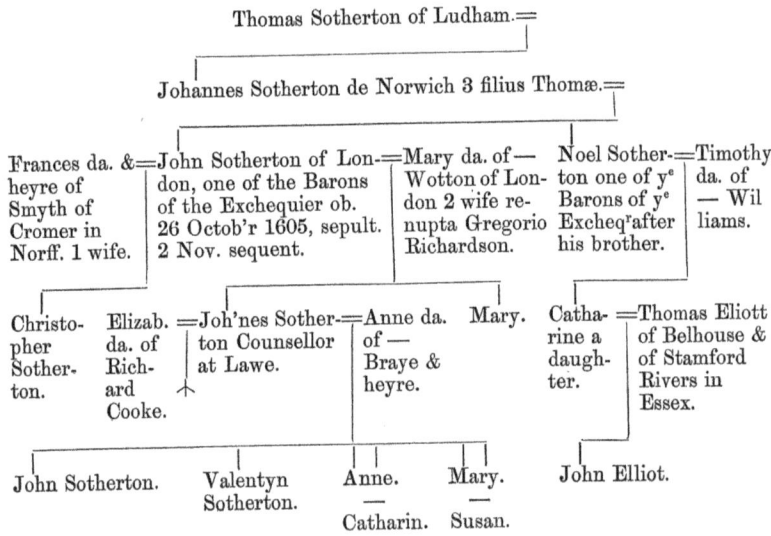

Johannes Sotherton de Norwich 3 filius Thomæ.=

Frances da. &=John Sotherton of Lon-=Mary da. of —   Noel Sother-=Timothy
heyre of   don, one of the Barons   Wotton of Lon- ton one of yᵉ | da. of
Smyth of   of the Exchequier ob.   don 2 wife re- Barons of yᵉ | — Wil
Cromer in   26 Octob'r 1605, sepult. nupta Gregorio Excheq'after | liams.
Norff. 1 wife. 2 Nov. sequent.   Richardson.   his brother.

Christo-   Elizab. =Joh'nes Sother-=Anne da.   Mary.   Catha- =Thomas Eliott
pher   da. of   ton Counsellor of —   rine a of Belhouse &
Sother-   Rich-   at Lawe.   Braye &   daugh- of Stamford
ton.   ard   heyre.   ter.   Rivers in
            Cooke.   Essex.

John Sotherton.   Valentyn   Anne.   Mary.   John Elliot.
                   Sotherton.   —   —
                                 Catharin. Susan.

Yorke.

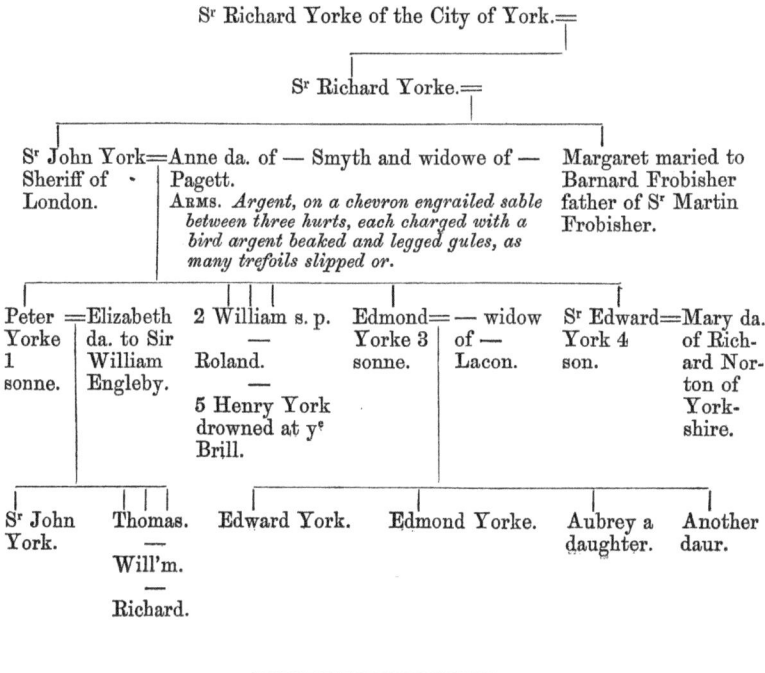

Sʳ Richard Yorke of the City of York.═

Sʳ Richard Yorke.═

Sʳ John York═Anne da. of — Smyth and widowe of —
Sheriff of   Pagett.
London.   ARMS. *Argent, on a chevron engrailed sable between three hurts, each charged with a bird argent beaked and legged gules, as many trefoils slipped or.*

Margaret maried to Barnard Frobisher father of Sʳ Martin Frobisher.

Peter ═Elizabeth   2 William s. p.   Edmond═— widow   Sʳ Edward═Mary da.
Yorke da. to Sir   Yorke 3 of —   York 4   of Rich-
1   William   Roland.   sonne.   Lacon.   son.   ard Nor-
sonne. Engleby.   —   ton of
                   5 Henry York   York-
                   drowned at yᵉ   shire.
                   Brill.

Sʳ John   Thomas.   Edward York.   Edmond Yorke.   Aubrey a   Another
York.   —   daughter.   daur.
           Will'm.
           —
           Richard.

Essex.

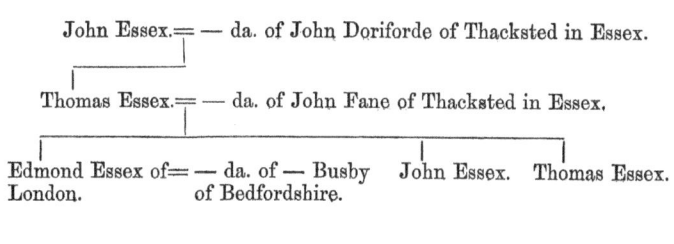

John Essex.═— da. of John Doriforde of Thacksted in Essex.

Thomas Essex.═— da. of John Fane of Thacksted in Essex.

Edmond Essex of═— da. of — Busby   John Essex.   Thomas Essex.
London.   of Bedfordshire.

M

Freare.

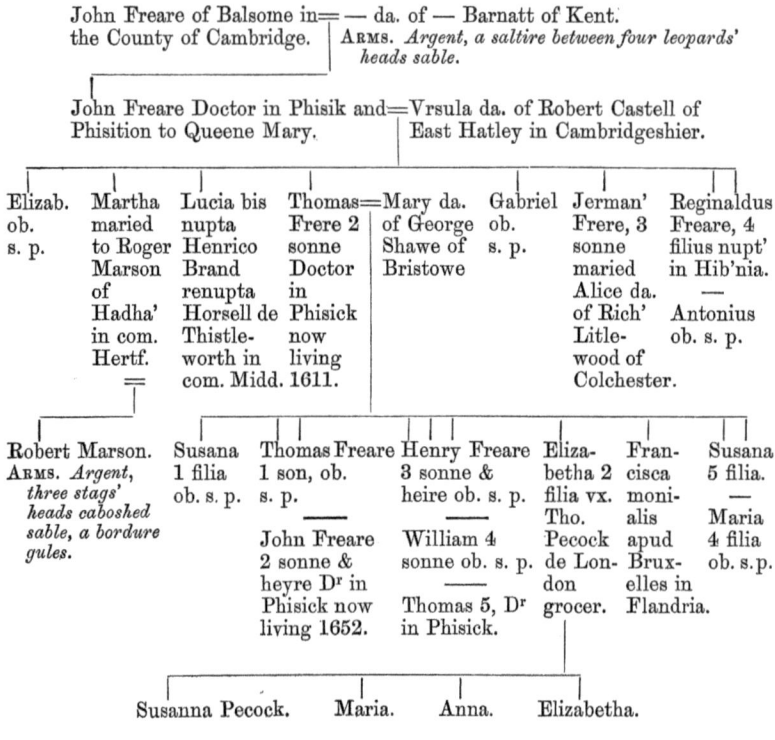

John Freare of Balsome in=—da. of — Barnatt of Kent.
the County of Cambridge. | ARMS. *Argent, a saltire between four leopards'*
heads sable.

John Freare Doctor in Phisik and=Vrsula da. of Robert Castell of
Phisition to Queene Mary. | East Hatley in Cambridgeshier.

| Elizab. ob. s. p. | Martha maried to Roger Marson of Hadha' in com. Hertf. | Lucia bis nupta Henrico Brand renupta Horsell de Thistleworth in com. Midd. | Thomas=Mary da. Frere 2 of George sonne Shawe of Doctor Bristowe in Phisick now living 1611. | Gabriel ob. s. p. | Jerman' Frere, 3 sonne maried Alice da. of Rich' Litlewood of Colchester. | Reginaldus Freare, 4 filius nupt' in Hib'nia. — Antonius ob. s. p. |

| Robert Marson. ARMS. *Argent, three stags' heads caboshed sable, a bordure gules.* | Susana 1 filia ob. s. p. — John Freare 2 sonne & heyre D' in Phisick now living 1652. | Thomas Freare 1 son, ob. s. p. | Henry Freare 3 sonne & heire ob. s. p. William 4 sonne ob. s. p. — Thomas 5, D' in Phisick. | Elizabetha 2 filia vx. Tho. Pecock de London grocer. | Francisca monialis apud Bruxelles in Flandria. | Susana 5 filia. — Maria 4 filia ob. s. p. |

Susanna Pecock.   Maria.   Anna.   Elizabetha.

Bullock.

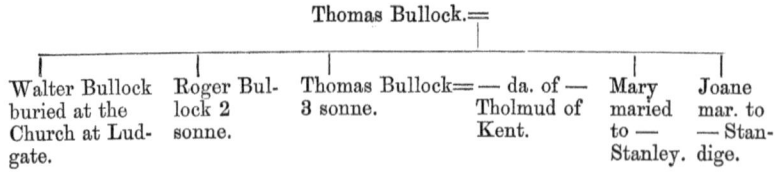

Thomas Bullock.=

| Walter Bullock buried at the Church at Ludgate. | Roger Bullock 2 sonne. | Thomas Bullock=—da. of — 3 sonne. Tholmud of Kent. | Mary maried to — Stanley. | Joane mar. to — Standige. |

Cowper.

ARMS. *Argent, on a bend engrailed between two lions rampant sable three plates.*
CREST. *A lion rampant sable, holding paleways a tilting spear argent.*

John Couper Esq[r] Seriant of Lawe borne at Horlye in y[e] County of Surrey 1539 maried Julian da. of Cuthbert Blackden Esq. w[ch] John was Seariantt at lawe but one yeare and half & died the 15 of March 1590, being of the age of 51 yeares and lieth buried at Cappell in Surrey.

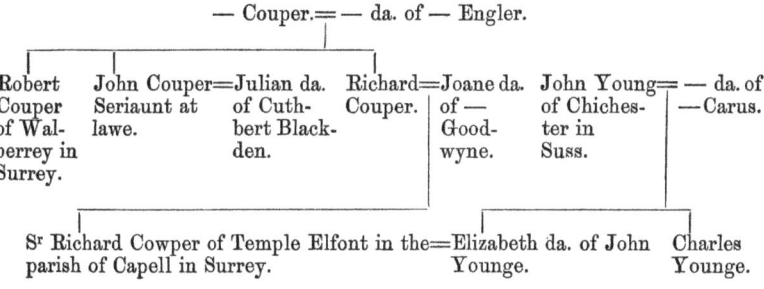

— Couper.= — da. of — Engler.

Robert Couper of Walberrey in Surrey.

John Couper Seriaunt at lawe. = Julian da. of Cuthbert Blackden.

Richard Couper. = Joane da. of — Goodwyne.

John Young = — da. of — Carus. of Chichester in Suss.

S[r] Richard Cowper of Temple Elfont in the parish of Capell in Surrey. = Elizabeth da. of John Younge.

Charles Younge.

Harborne.

ARMS. *Gules, on a fess or between three bezants a lion passant sable, a crescent for difference.*
CREST. *A bezant between two lions' gambs sable.*

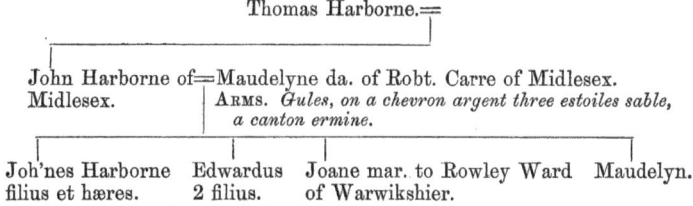

Thomas Harborne.=

John Harborne of Midlesex. = Maudelyne da. of Robt. Carre of Midlesex.
ARMS. *Gules, on a chevron argent three estoiles sable, a canton ermine.*

Joh'nes Harborne filius et hæres.

Edwardus 2 filius.

Joane mar. to Rowley Ward of Warwikshier.

Maudelyn.

William Harborne of Yarmouth (bears), *Gules, on a fess or between three bezants a lion passant sable, impaling argent on a chief vert a cross tau between two mullets or.* (DRURY.)
CREST. *On a cap of maintenance sable, turned up ermine, an eagle displayed or.*

Stile.

ARMS. *Sable, a fess or fretty of the field between three fleurs-de-lis within a bordure of the second.*

Sir Guy Wolston Knt 19 E. IV. =

Margareta filia & cohæres nupta = Guidoni Saboote militi.

John Stile of Langley in yᵉ p'ish of = Eliz. da. & coheyre of Sir Guy Wolston qui fuit sup'stes 19 E. 4. Beckenham in Kent.

ARMS. *Quarterly:—1 and 4. Argent, a wolf passant sable. 2. Argent, three turnstiles sable, a mullet for difference. 3. Argent, on a chevron sable between three rams' heads erased azure, as many billets or.*

Anna vx. Jo. Broughton militis; renupta Joh'ni com. Bedford.

Eliz. vx. Joh'is Stile renupta Jacobo Yarford militi.

Brigida nupta Edm'o Kempe civi London nato in Suff.

Florencia nupta Rob'to Robinson de Boston.

Eliz. f. Geo. = Sr Humfrey Stile of Peryn vx. Langley sonne & heyre, 2. Kt p. H. 8 at his going to Bullen.

= Briget da. to Sr Tho. Baldry maior of London.

Joh'nes s. p.

Oliver Stile = Susan da. of — Bull 2 sonne and Sheriff of London.

ARMS. *Argent, on a canton sable a lion's head erased or.*

Nicholas = Gertrude da. of — Stile 4 Bright of London. sonne Sheriff of London.

Edw. s. p.

ARMS. *Sable, on a bend between three mullets two and one argent, three crosses crosslet fitché of the field.*

Maria vx. Simonis Lawrence

Humfridus Stile.

Thomas Stile of Watringbury in Kent. =

C

Maria vx. Xpoferi Meade de com. Warr.

Edmond sonne & = Mary da. of heyre of Sr Humfrey Stile Knight & Briget his wife, of Langley.

John Berney of Redham in Norff. Esq.

Julian da. of — Barnes 2 wife.

Margareta vx. Georgii Needham de com. Hertf.

Edmond = Catherina da. of Jo. Stile. Scott of Kent.

ARMS. *Three catherine wheels within a bordure engrailed.*

Edwardus ob. iuvenis s. p.

William Stile = Mary da. of Sir son & heyre Rob. Clark of Langley. Baron of yᵉ Exchequer.

Anne sole da. of = John Eversfield of Sussex Esq. ali' Ersfeild.

Anna vx. Georgii Franklyn de com. Bedf.

A

B

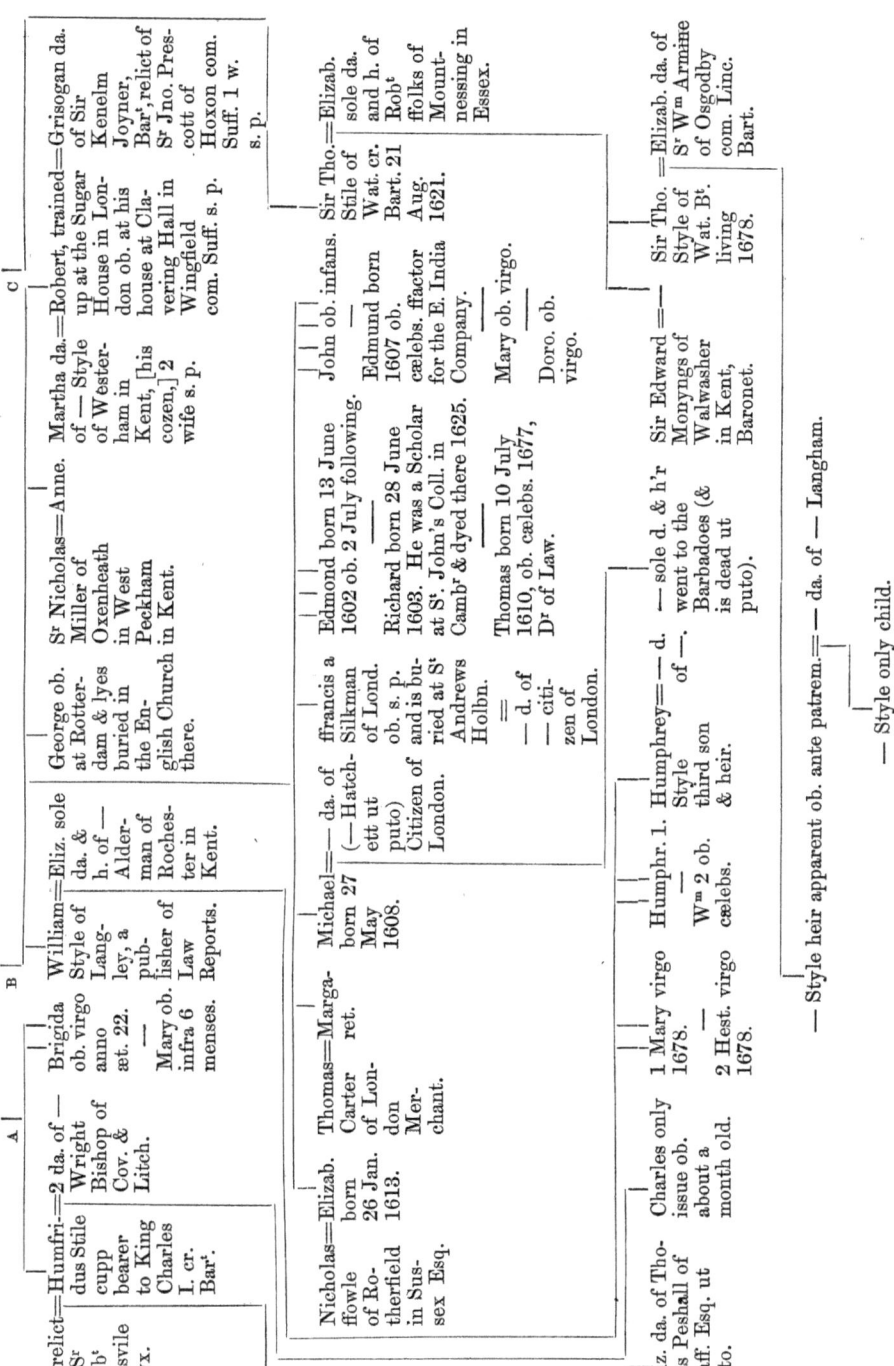

𝕳𝖆𝖗𝖇𝖞𝖊.

ARMS. *Gules, a fess dancetté ermine between ten billets argent, four in chief, three, two, and one in base, a mullet for difference.*

CREST. *A heron's head erased or, beaked sable, between two wings expanded of the last bezanté.*

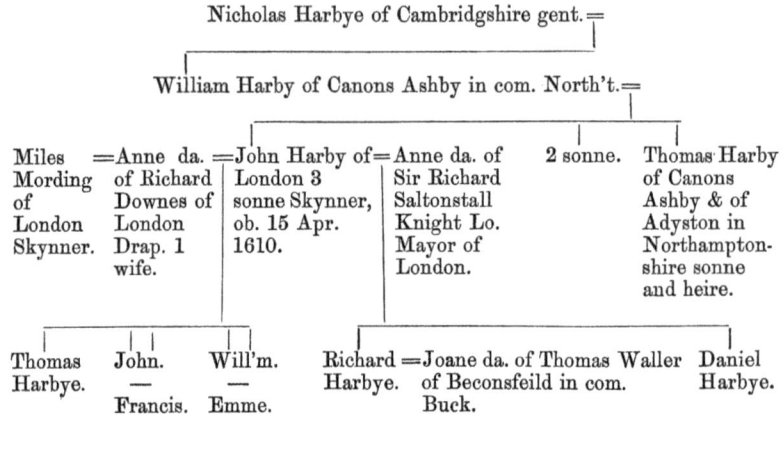

Nicholas Harbye of Cambridgshire gent.=

William Harby of Canons Ashby in com. North't.=

| Miles Mording of London Skynner. | =Anne da. of Richard Downes of London Drap. 1 wife. | =John Harby of London 3 sonne Skynner, ob. 15 Apr. 1610. | =Anne da. of Sir Richard Saltonstall Knight Lo. Mayor of London. | 2 sonne. | Thomas Harby of Canons Ashby & of Adyston in Northampton-shire sonne and heire. |

| Thomas Harbye. | John. — Francis. | Will'm. — Emme. | Richard Harbye. | =Joane da. of Thomas Waller of Beconsfeild in com. Buck. | Daniel Harbye. |

𝕾𝖐𝖞𝖓𝖓𝖊𝖗.

ARMS. *(Argent), on a fess between three lures (gules) a lion passant (of the field).*

This epitaphe taken from of his toombe.

Here lieth yᵉ Corpes of Thomas Skynner late Citizen and Alderman of Londo' borne at Saffron Walden in Essex, who in the 65 yeare of his age, and on yᵉ 30 day of Dece'br Aº Dni 1596 being then Lo. Mayor of this Citye dep'ted this life leauing behinde him 3 sonnes and 3 daughters.

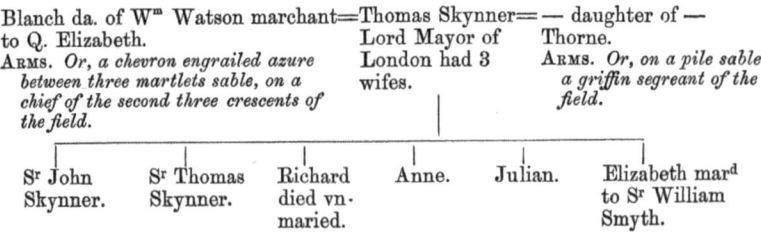

| Blanch da. of Wᵐ Watson marchant to Q. Elizabeth. ARMS. *Or, a chevron engrailed azure between three martlets sable, on a chief of the second three crescents of the field.* | =Thomas Skynner= Lord Mayor of London had 3 wifes. | — daughter of — Thorne. ARMS. *Or, on a pile sable a griffin segreant of the field.* |

| Sʳ John Skynner. | Sʳ Thomas Skynner. | Richard died vn-maried. | Anne. | Julian. | Elizabeth marᵈ to Sʳ William Smyth. |

Gardner.

ARMS. *Azure, a griffin passant or.*
CREST. *On a ducal coronet a lion passant guardant argent.*
ANOTHER. *A demi-unicorn erased, crowned and horned or, crined sable.*

William Gardenor of Hartfordshier.═Eliz. daughter of — Michell his wife.

| Richard Gardner sergeant at Armes to King H. 8. ob. s. p. | Margaret da. of — wife to — Roderey after to Frement Abraham hosier at Newgate. | ═William Gardner of Bermondsey Street obijt 1597. | ═Frances da. of Robert Lucy, first wife. | Friswold a da. maried to — English sergeant of the Bakehouse ; after to — Askewe & lastly to — Sheppard. |

| Christo-═Judith pher Sakvile Gardi- da. to ner my Lord dyed of Buk-1596. hurstes vncle. | 3. Richard ob. s. p. | 2. Thomas═— da. of Gardner. — Skipwith of St Albons. | William Gardner 3 sonne. ═ Mary da. of Xpofer Yelverton. | Catarine maried to John Stepkyn ; after to Nicolas Smyth.═ | Anne mar. to Simon Perrott of Staff. and Warrwickshier.═ |

| Christopher Gardner sonne and heyre. — Francis. | William Gardner. — Francis. | Margaret. — Catarin. | Xpofer Smyth. — Francis. — John. | William. — | Will'm Perrott. — Simon. | Dorothy. — Frances. — Vrsula. |

Baron.

ARMS. *Per fess azure and gules, two lions passant guardant argent, collared counter-changed.*

Concess. præfato Thomæ p' Rob. Cook Clarenceux post mortem in funere vtenda et suis in p'petuum.

Anna filia Thomæ Aphowell de═Thomas Baron alias Barne de═Anna filia Rob'ti
Com. Monmouth in Wallia.   Alborough hache in p'ochia   Brokesby de
ARMS. *Argent, a lion rampant*   de Barking in Essex died at   comitatu Lin-
sable debruised by a fess   his howse in London 29 Junii   colniæ vxor
engrailed gules.   1573 & buried at Barking in   prima.
                         Essex.

| Paulus Baron 3 filius. | Thomas Baron filius et hæres æt. 28 annor. | Barthus Baron ob. s. p. | Anna. |

Romney.

ARMS. *Azure, on a bend cotised argent three escallops gules.*

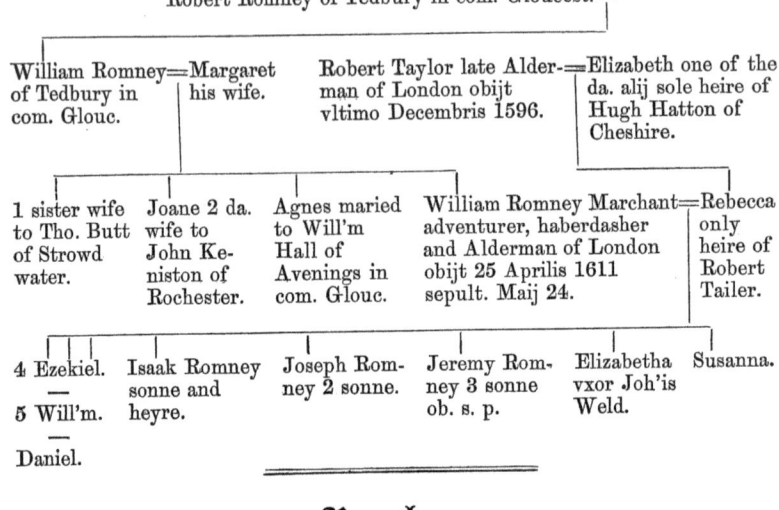

Robert Romney of Tedbury in com. Gloucest.⹀

William Romney⹀Margaret his wife.
of Tedbury in
com. Glouc.

Robert Taylor late Alder-⹀Elizabeth one of the
man of London obijt | da. alij sole heire of
vltimo Decembris 1596. | Hugh Hatton of
Cheshire.

1 sister wife to Tho. Butt of Strowd water.

Joane 2 da. wife to John Keniston of Rochester.

Agnes maried to Will'm Hall of Avenings in com. Glouc.

William Romney Marchant⹀Rebecca
adventurer, haberdasher | only
and Alderman of London | heire of
obijt 25 Aprilis 1611 | Robert
sepult. Maij 24. | Tailer.

4 Ezekiel.
—
5 Will'm.
—
Daniel.

Isaak Romney sonne and heyre.

Joseph Romney 2 sonne.

Jeremy Romney 3 sonne ob. s. p.

Elizabetha vxor Joh'is Weld.

Susanna.

Barnham.

ARMS. *Quarterly :—1 and 4. Sable, a cross engrailed between four crescents argent.
2 and 3. Azure, a pheon argent.* (BRADBRIDGE.)

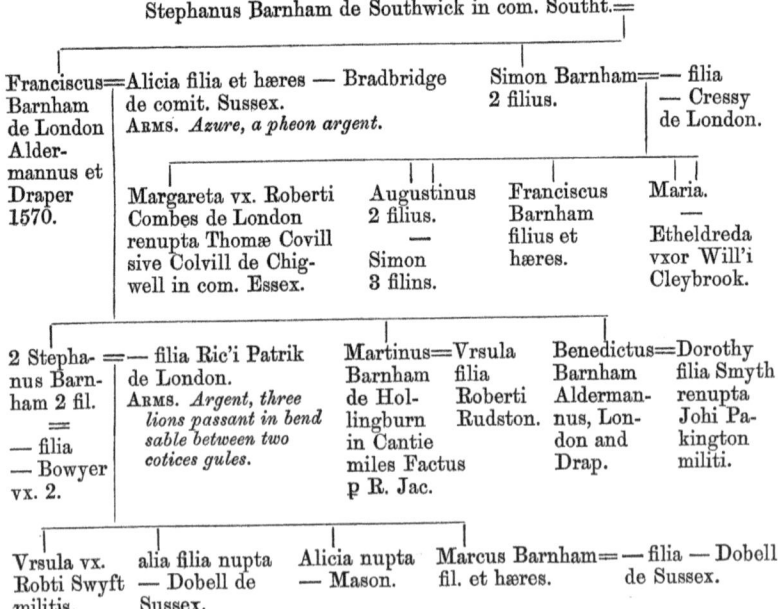

Stephanus Barnham de Southwick in com. Southt.⹀

Franciscus⹀Alicia filia et hæres — Bradbridge
Barnham | de comit. Sussex.
de London | ARMS. *Azure, a pheon argent.*
Alder-
mannus et
Draper
1570.

Simon Barnham⹀— filia
2 filius. | — Cressy
| de London.

Margareta vx. Roberti
Combes de London
renupta Thomæ Covill
sive Colvill de Chig-
well in com. Essex.

Augustinus
2 filius.
—
Simon
3 filins.

Franciscus
Barnham
filius et
hæres.

Maria.
—
Etheldreda
vxor Will'i
Cleybrook.

2 Stepha-⹀— filia Ric'i Patrik
nus Barn- | de London.
ham 2 fil. | ARMS. *Argent, three
= | lions passant in bend
— filia | sable between two
— Bowyer | cotices gules.*
vx. 2.

Martinus⹀Vrsula
Barnham | filia
de Hol- | Roberti
lingburn | Rudston.
in Cantie
miles Factus
p R. Jac.

Benedictus⹀Dorothy
Barnham | filia Smyth
Alderman- | renupta
nus, Lon- | Johi Pa-
don and | kington
Drap. | militi.

Vrsula vx.
Robti Swyft
militis.

alia filia nupta
— Dobell de
Sussex.

Alicia nupta
— Mason.

Marcus Barnham⹀— filia — Dobell
fil. et hæres. | de Sussex.

Dene.

ARMS. *Gules, a lion sejant guardant or, on a chief argent three crescents of the field.*
CREST. *A demi-lion rampant guardant or, holding a crescent gules.*

Concess. p' Wm Dethik Garter & Wm Camden Clarenceux.

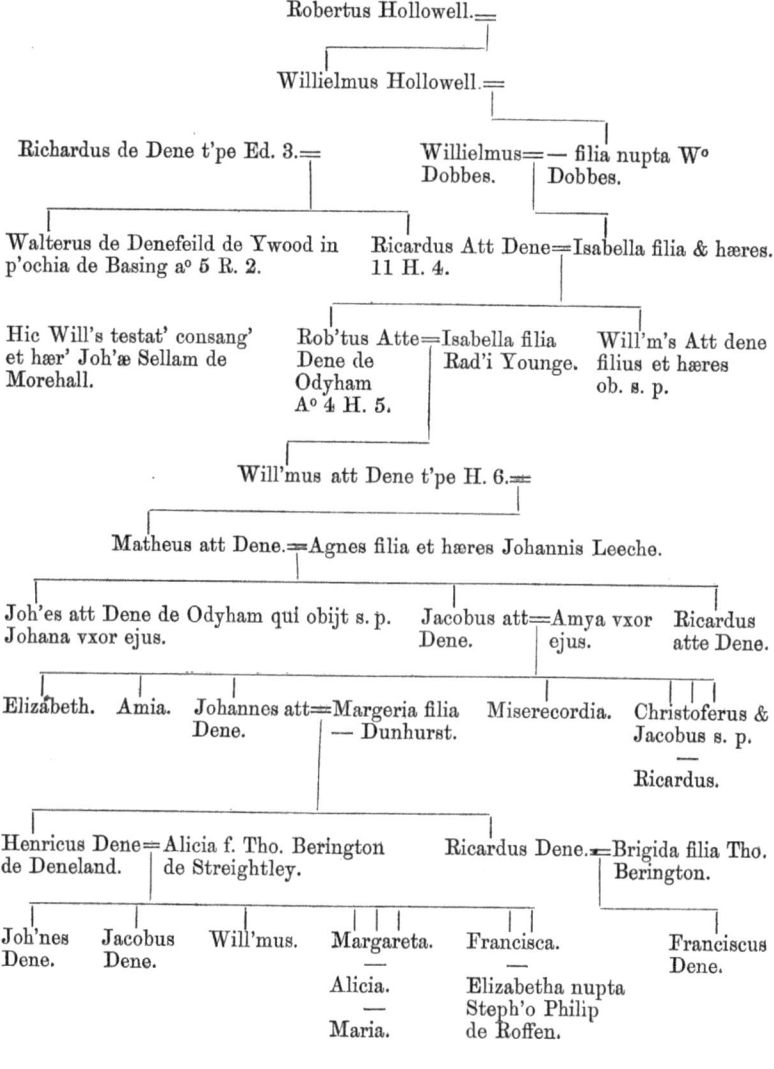

Robertus Hollowell.=

Willielmus Hollowell.=

Richardus de Dene t'pe Ed. 3.=

Willielmus=— filia nupta W°
Dobbes. | Dobbes.

Walterus de Denefeild de Ywood in
p'ochia de Basing a° 5 R. 2.

Ricardus Att Dene=Isabella filia & hæres.
11 H. 4.

Hic Will's testat' consang'
et hær' Joh'æ Sellam de
Morehall.

Rob'tus Atte=Isabella filia
Dene de | Rad'i Younge.
Odyham
A° 4 H. 5.

Will'm's Att dene
filius et hæres
ob. s. p.

Will'mus att Dene t'pe H. 6.==

Matheus att Dene.==Agnes filia et hæres Johannis Leeche.

Joh'es att Dene de Odyham qui obijt s. p.
Johana vxor ejus.

Jacobus att=Amya vxor
Dene. | ejus.

Ricardus
atte Dene.

Elizabeth. Amia. Johannes att==Margeria filia
Dene. | — Dunhurst.

Miserecordia.

Christoferus &
Jacobus s. p.
—
Ricardus.

Henricus Dene==Alicia f. Tho. Berington
de Deneland. | de Streightley.

Ricardus Dene.==Brigida filia Tho.
Berington.

Joh'nes Jacobus Will'mus. Margareta.
Dene. Dene. —
Alicia.
—
Maria.

Francisca.
—
Elizabetha nupta
Steph'o Philip
de Roffen.

Franciscus
Dene.

Searle.

ARMS. *Gules, on a chevron between three trefoils argent as many ogresses.*
CREST. *A demi-lion rampant or, holding a broken mast sable, the top set off with palisadoes, thereon a flag argent charged with a cross gules.*

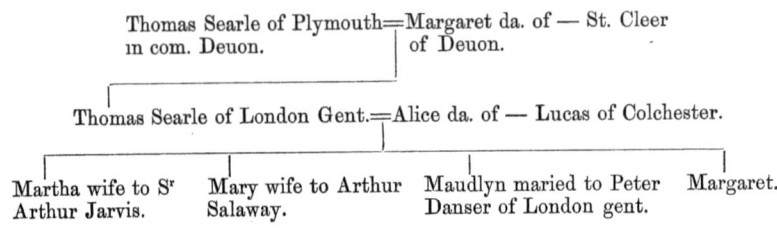

Thomas Searle of Plymouth=Margaret da. of — St. Cleer
in com. Deuon. | of Deuon.

Thomas Searle of London Gent.=Alice da. of — Lucas of Colchester.

Martha wife to S* Arthur Jarvis.   Mary wife to Arthur Salaway.   Maudlyn maried to Peter Danser of London gent.   Margaret.

Naylour.

ARMS. *Or, a pale between two lions rampant sable.*
CREST. *A lion's head erased sable, charged on the neck with a saltire or.*

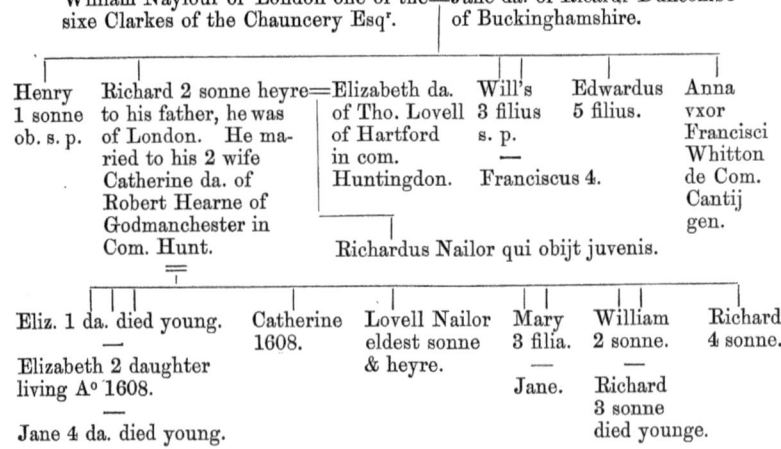

William Naylour of London one of the=Jane da. of Ricardi Duncombe
sixe Clarkes of the Chauncery Esqr. | of Buckinghamshire.

Henry 1 sonne ob. s. p.   Richard 2 sonne heyre=Elizabeth da. of Tho. Lovell of Hartford in com. Huntingdon.
to his father, he was of London. He maried to his 2 wife Catherine da. of Robert Hearne of Godmanchester in Com. Hunt.
  Will's 3 filius s. p. — Franciscus 4.   Edwardus 5 filius.   Anna vxor Francisci Whitton de Com. Cantij gen.

Richardus Nailor qui obijt juvenis.

Eliz. 1 da. died young.

Elizabeth 2 daughter living Aº 1608.

Jane 4 da. died young.

Catherine 1608.

Lovell Nailor eldest sonne & heyre.

Mary 3 filia. — Jane.

William 2 sonne — Richard 3 sonne died younge.

Richard 4 sonne.

Baron.

ARMS. *Azure, two lions passant guardant argent.*

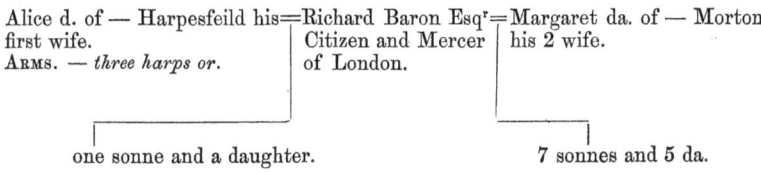

Alice d. of — Harpesfeild his=Richard Baron Esqr=Margaret da. of — Morton
first wife.   Citizen and Mercer | his 2 wife.
ARMS. — *three harps or.*   of London.

one sonne and a daughter.   7 sonnes and 5 da.

Weld.

ARMS. *Quarterly :—1 and 4. Azure, a fess nebulé between three crescents ermine.
2. . . . three lions rampant . . . a chief . . .   4. . . . three chevrons, each charged
with a roundle . . .*

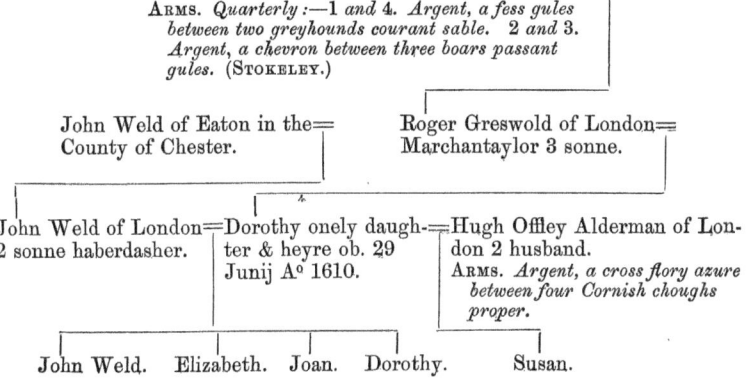

Richard Greswold of Solihull in com. Warr. Ar.=
ARMS. *Quarterly :—1 and 4. Argent, a fess gules
between two greyhounds courant sable. 2 and 3.
Argent, a chevron between three boars passant
gules.* (STOKELEY.)

John Weld of Eaton in the=   Roger Greswold of London=
County of Chester.   Marchantaylor 3 sonne.

John Weld of London=Dorothy onely daugh-=Hugh Offley Alderman of Lon-
2 sonne haberdasher.   ter & heyre ob. 29   don 2 husband.
             Junij A^o 1610.   ARMS. *Argent, a cross flory azure
                              between four Cornish choughs
                              proper.*

John Weld.   Elizabeth.   Joan.   Dorothy.   Susan.

Cordell.

ARMS. *Gules, a chevron engrailed between three griffins' heads erased ermine.*
CREST. *A cockatrice, wings close vert, wattled beaked and collared or.*

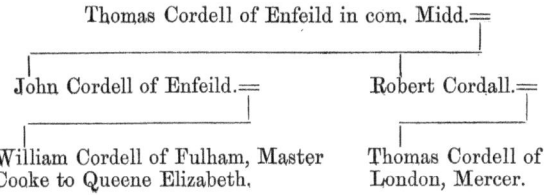

Thomas Cordell of Enfeild in com. Midd.=

John Cordell of Enfeild.=   Robert Cordall.=

William Cordell of Fulham, Master   Thomas Cordell of
Cooke to Queene Elizabeth.   London, Mercer.

Treswell.

ARMS. *Argent, three mullets pierced gules between two bendlets sable.*

— Treswell of St Albons t'pe Edw. 4.=   Radulfus Friday miles.=

Richard Treswell alias =Joane da. of —   Langley.=   Roger=Isabell
Baker of Kings Lang-   Carter of Chip-   Petre. | Fryday.
ley in com. Hert. after   ford in the p'ish
of the Bakehouse.   of Kings Langley.
sepult apud Kings
Langley.

John Treswell   Rafe Baker   William   Rob't =Margaret   Anne   =Rogerus
alias Baker 1   2 sonne.   Baker of   Tres-   da. of —   another   Petre.
sonne.   —   Barn-   well   Langley.   da. of   =
=   Robt.   hay.   alias   Langley.   Margarett.
Margaret da.   Baker of   Baker
of — Bury of   Kings   of St Will'm   Hugh   Mary   Elizab.
Abbots   Langley 3   Al-   Peter   Peter   Peter   Peter.
Langley.   sonne.   bons   s. p.   s. p.   s. p.
                                    5
                                   sonne.

Nicholas = — da.   Anne da. of — Calthrop,=Radulphus Tres-=Cicely   Joane
Treswell. | of —   widow of Robt. Kentish   well de S^t da. of   maried
       | Jones.   2 wife ob. s. p.   Albons & Citi-   — Cres-   to —
               ARMS. *Quarterly :*—1 *and*   zen of London   ley 1   Dy-
                 6. *Chequy or and azure,*   mar. to his 3   wife.   banke.
Cecily.   Hugh   Mar-   *a fess ermine.* 2. *Gules,*   wife Eliz. da. of   =
—   Tres-   gery   *on a chief argent two*   — Swanson &
Anne.   well.   wife   *mullets sable.* BACON.   widow of Ed-   Elen.   Thomas
              of —   3. *Azure, three griffins*   ward Bachelor.   Dybank.
              Price.   *passant in pale or.* WITHE.   —
                 4. *Azure, a fess between six*   Mary.
                 crosses crosslet or. ST.
                 OMER.   5. *Argent, a lion*
                 rampant sable, STAPLETON.

Anne   =Robert Treswell   =Mary da. of   Rafe Tres-=Susan da.   Christofer
daugh-   Somersett herald   William Castle   well 2   of —   Treswell
ter of   of Armes Esqr of the County   sonne.   Peterson.   3 sonne.
Rich-   mar. to his first   of Huntingdon
ard   wife Susa' da. of   3 wife. sepulta
Gad-   Andrew Lyons   in eccl'ia S'ci   Rafe.   Susan.   Robert   Anne·
bury 2   who died with-   Botolphi extra   Treswell.   —
wife.   out issue 23   Aldersgate A^o Elizab.   Mary.   Ann.
         Dec. 1590.   D^o 1613, 20   all died young, s. p.
                            Ap^r.

Robert   Robt 2 sonne   Joyce.   Andrew   Francis   Lucia.   John Tres-
Treswell   died young.   —   Treswell   Tres-   well 3
3 sonne.   Susan.   1 sonne   well 4   sonne.
                         & heyre.   sonne.

Freeman.

ARMS. *Azure, three lozenges argent, in chief a crescent or.*
CREST. *A demi-lion rampant (gules) charged with a lozenge (or).*

Martin Freeman of London=Elizabeth da. of Mathew Laurence; 2 sonne of
sonne of Edm. of Hanning- | Sr Oliuer Laurence.
ton in com. Northamp. | ARMS. *Quarterly :—1 and 4. Argent, a cross ragulé*
| *gules. 2 and 3. Argent, two bars and in chief*
| *three mullets gules.* WASHINGTON.

Ralphe Freeman sonne and heyre ætatis 27 annor 1616. Lo. Mayor of London A° 1633.	Will'm 2 sonne. Martin 3 sonne.	John 4 sonne. Francis 5 sonne.	James 6 sonne.	Elizabeth wiffe of Stephen Haruey of London.=

Martin æt 6 annor'.   Elizabeth 2 annor'.

Le Maire.

ARMS. *Quarterly :—1. Argent, three moors' heads couped proper. 2. Gules, three*
boars' heads argent. (BARY.) *3. Gules, a chevron between three lozenges*
argent. 4. Erminois, a crescent sable. 5. Argent, a bend lozengy gules, in
chief an escallop azure. 6. Or, a martlet sable.
CREST. *A moor's head couped proper, wreathed argent.*
MOTTO. *Tempera te tempori.*

Jacobus Le Maire=Catharina filia et hæres Petri de Bary de St Brixe ex Catha-
de Turnay. | rina filia et hæres de Bonenfant.
| ARMS. *Quarterly :—1 and 6. Gules, three boars' heads argent. 2.*
| *Gules, a chevron between three lozenges argent. 3. Erminois, a*
| *crescent sable. 4. Argent, a bend lozengy gules, in chief an*
| *escallop azure. 5. Or, a martlet sable.*

David Le Maire=Sara filia Petri Trian de London.
de London. | ARMS. *Argent, a fess embattled between six estoiles or.*

Henricus Swin-=Maria filia nerton de Lon- prima don prim' Davidis le maritus. Maire. ARMS. *Quarterly :—* 1 and 4. Argent, a cross flory sable. 2 and 3. Argent, a cross flory sable within a bordure engrailed gules.	=Franciscus Crane de Mortlack in com. Surr' miles 2 vx. ARMS. *Per bend or and azure.*	Petrus Le Maire miles filius et hæres.	Edward Baeshe= de Stansted in comitatu Hart- ford mil. ARMS. *Per chevron argent and gules, in chief two cocks sable, in base a saltire or.*	=Sara filia Davidi Le Maire.

Baron.

ARMS. *Azure, two lions passant guardant argent.*
CREST. *Out of clouds argent a dexter arm in armour erect, couped at the elbow, holding in the gauntlet or a broken sword of the last, the blade proper.*

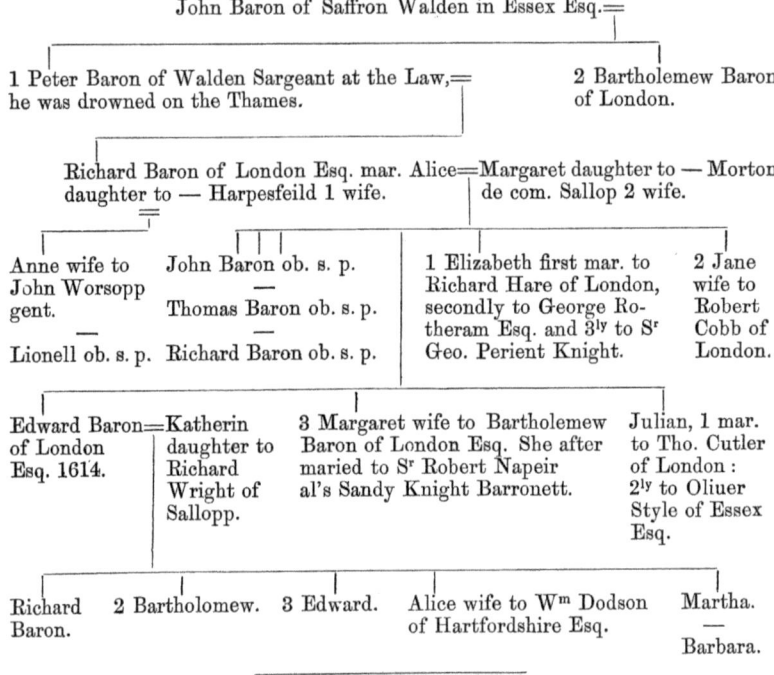

John Baron of Saffron Walden in Essex Esq.=

1 Peter Baron of Walden Sargeant at the Law,=
he was drowned on the Thames.

2 Bartholemew Baron of London.

Richard Baron of London Esq. mar. Alice=Margaret daughter to — Morton
daughter to — Harpesfeild 1 wife. | de com. Sallop 2 wife.

Anne wife to John Worsopp gent.
—
Lionell ob. s. p.

John Baron ob. s. p.
—
Thomas Baron ob. s. p.
—
Richard Baron ob. s. p.

1 Elizabeth first mar. to Richard Hare of London, secondly to George Rotheram Esq. and 3ly to Sr Geo. Perient Knight.

2 Jane wife to Robert Cobb of London.

Edward Baron=Katherin
of London | daughter to
Esq. 1614. | Richard
| Wright of
| Sallopp.

3 Margaret wife to Bartholemew Baron of London Esq. She after maried to Sr Robert Napeir al's Sandy Knight Barronett.

Julian, 1 mar. to Tho. Cutler of London : 2ly to Oliuer Style of Essex Esq.

Richard Baron.

2 Bartholomew.

3 Edward.

Alice wife to Wm Dodson of Hartfordshire Esq.

Martha.
—
Barbara.

Dale.

ARMS. *Gules, on a mount vert a swan argent, membered and ducally gorged or.*
CREST. *On a chapeau . . . turned up ermine, a stork argent, beaked legged and ducally gorged or.*

This armes and creast was confirmed to William Dale
of Brigstock and of London A° 1613.

Robert Dale of Wencle in Prestbury in com. Chester.=Katherin daughter of —

1 Robert Dale of Wincle.

2 Roger Dale of The Inner Temple.

3 William Dale of London=Elizabeth daughter
and of Brigstock in com. | of Tho. Elliott of
Northamp. Esq. | Surrey Esqr.

Robert Dale of Wincle.

Roger Dale.

Robert Dale son and heire.

Mary.

Elizabeth.

Agnes.

Joane.

Morgan.

ARMS. *Quarterly :—1 and 4. Or, a fess wavy and in chief two eagles displayed sable.*
2 and 3. Barry of twelve or and azure. (COPCOTT.)
CREST. *An eagle displayed or, charged on the breast with a fess wavy sable.*

This Armes and Creast was confirmed by M[r] William Dethick Garter A[o] 1588 to
Hugh Morgan, and sithence the same was confirmed by M[r] Camden Clar. in
A[o] 1613 to Robert Morgan nephew & heire of the saied Hugh.

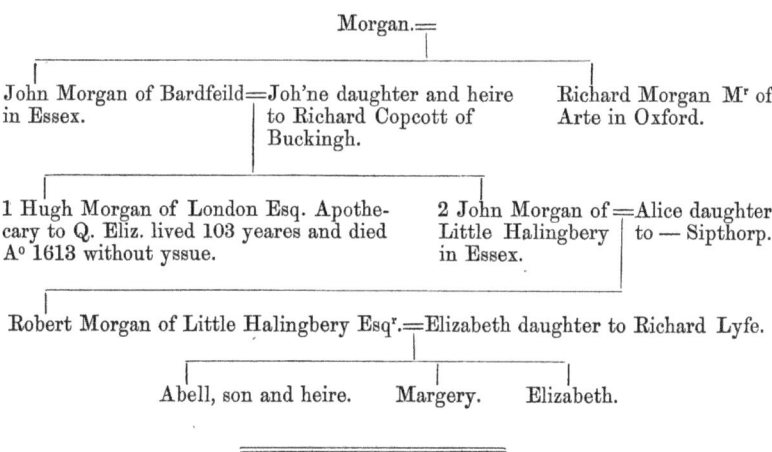

Morgan.=

John Morgan of Bardfeild=Joh'ne daughter and heire to Richard Copcott of Buckingh. in Essex.

Richard Morgan M[r] of Arte in Oxford.

1 Hugh Morgan of London Esq. Apothecary to Q. Eliz. lived 103 yeares and died A[o] 1613 without yssue.

2 John Morgan of Little Halingbery in Essex.=Alice daughter to — Sipthorp.

Robert Morgan of Little Halingbery Esq[r].=Elizabeth daughter to Richard Lyfe.

Abell, son and heire.   Margery.   Elizabeth.

Gabott.

Robert Gabot of Acton Burnell in the County of Sallop had this Banner giuen=
him by Maximilian the Emperor for his Seruice (viz.)
Gules, a griffin segreant or, holding in his claws a flagstaff bendy argent and sable, on
it a flag of the third charged with a double-headed eagle displayed of the second.

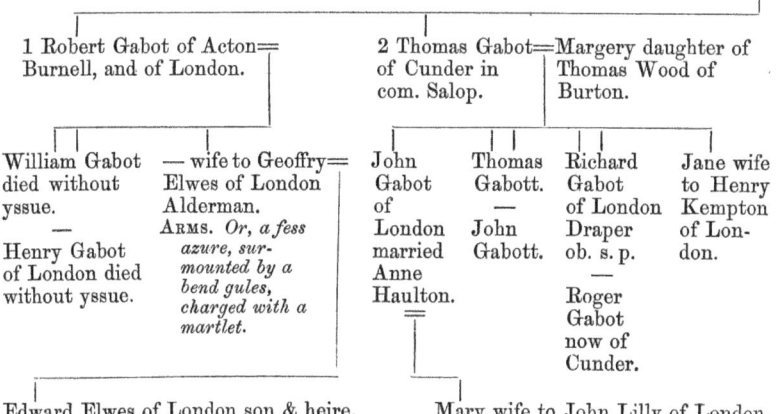

1 Robert Gabot of Acton=Burnell, and of London.

2 Thomas Gabot=Margery daughter of of Cunder in com. Salop. Thomas Wood of Burton.

William Gabot died without yssue.
—
Henry Gabot of London died without yssue.

— wife to Geoffry=Elwes of London Alderman.
ARMS. *Or, a fess azure, surmounted by a bend gules, charged with a martlet.*

John Gabot of London married Anne Haulton.
=

Thomas Gabott.
—
John Gabott.

Richard Gabot of London Draper ob. s. p.

Roger Gabot now of Cunder.

Jane wife to Henry Kempton of London.

Edward Elwes of London son & heire.

Mary wife to John Lilly of London.

Allaunson of London.

ARMS. *Quarterly :—1 and 4. (Argent) a fess (azure) between three boars' heads couped (sable). 2 and 3. . . . three covered cups, two and one . . . ; over all a martlet for difference ; impaling (gules) a chevron ermine between three round buckles (or), in chief a mullet for difference.* (DALBY.)
CREST. *A pheon (argent), in it a broken staff-handle (or), charged with a martlet for difference. Another : A mule's head erased.*

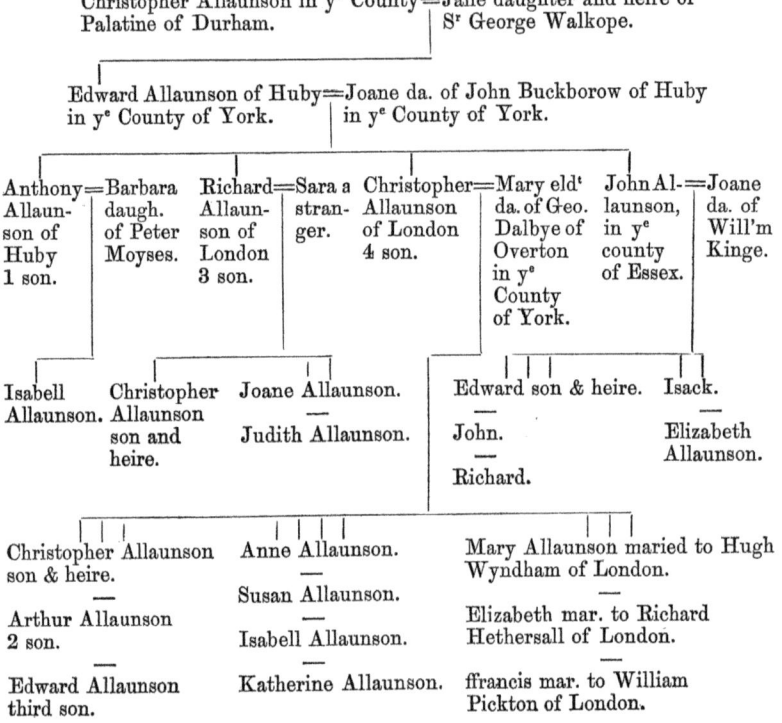

Christopher Allaunson in yᵉ County=Jane daughter and heire of
Palatine of Durham. | Sʳ George Walkope.

Edward Allaunson of Huby=Joane da. of John Buckborow of Huby
in yᵉ County of York. | in yᵉ County of York.

Anthony=Barbara   Richard=Sara a   Christopher=Mary eldᵗ   John Al-=Joane
Allaun- daugh.   Allaun- stran-   Allaunson   da. of Geo. launson, da. of
son of   of Peter son of   ger.   of London   Dalbye of   in yᵉ   Will'm
Huby   Moyses.   London   4 son.   Overton   county   Kinge.
1 son.   3 son.   in yᵉ   of Essex.
                                                  County
                                                  of York.

Isabell   Christopher   Joane Allaunson.   Edward son & heire.   Isack.
Allaunson. Allaunson
            son and   Judith Allaunson.   John.   Elizabeth
            heire.   Allaunson.
                                                Richard.

Christopher Allaunson   Anne Allaunson.   Mary Allaunson maried to Hugh
son & heire.   Wyndham of London.
                         Susan Allaunson.
Arthur Allaunson   Elizabeth mar. to Richard
2 son.   Isabell Allaunson. Hethersall of London.

Edward Allaunson   Katherine Allaunson.   ffrancis mar. to William
third son.   Pickton of London.

Vernon of London the blind Marchant Stapler who died Noue'br 1616 sine prole a great benefactour to the Marchant Tailors company.

ARMS. *Or, on a fess azure three garbs of the field, in chief two mullets gules.*
CREST. *A stag sejant or.*

Ferrers of London Lynnen draper.

ARMS. *Argent, on a bend gules cotised azure three horse-shoes or.*
CREST. *An ostrich proper, holding in the beak a horse-shoe or.*

Sʳ John King of London.

ARMS. *Sable, a lion passant or, a label of three points argent.*
CREST. *On a ducal coronet a lion rampant or, holding in his paw a lance argent on the point thereof an annulet or.*

Robynson of London Cheif wayter of the Custome howse.

ARMS. *Vert, on a chevron between three stags statant or, as many trefoils gules; impaling Quarterly:—1 and 4. Sable, a chevron ermine between three rams' heads erased argent. 2 and 3. Argent, a lion rampant sable, surmounted by a fess engrailed gules.*
CREST. *A stag statant or, pelletté.*

Gomersall of London.

ARMS. *Sable, a chevron engrailed ermine between three dexter gauntlets argent.*
CREST. *On a crescent or, a dexter gauntlet argent, grasping a battle-axe gules, pointed and headed of the second.*

Given by Sʳ Gilbt. Dethick Garter.

Cooper of London dwelling in Cornhill by the Exchange buried 13 of June 1609.

ARMS. *Argent, three martlets gules, on a chief engrailed of the second three annulets or, a crescent for difference; impaling sable, a fess dancetté argent, in chief two chaplets or.*

Borlacy of London.

ARMS. *Quarterly:—1 and 4. Or, three pales sable, fretty of the field. 2 and 3. Gules, three castles argent, and as many lions issuing therefrom or.*
CREST. *A stag's head erased proper, holding in his mouth a ribbon with the motto, " SPES MEA DEVS," thereon.*

Doctor Mountford of London the Phisicion.

ARMS. *Argent, three fleurs-de-lis gules, a martlet for difference; impaling gules, a chevron ermine between three garbs or.*

William Thwaytes of London Alderman 1597.

ARMS. *Argent, a cross sable fretty of the field, in the first quarter a fleur-de-lis gules.*
CREST. *A gamecock proper, beaked and wattled gules, charged on the breast with a fleur-de-lis of the last.*

p' Wᵐ Dethick Garter & Wᵐ Camden Clarenc. 1597.

Sʳ James Deane Knight of London.

ARMS. *Gules, a lion sejant guardant or, on a chief argent three crescents gules.*
CREST. *A demi-lion rampant, holding in his dexter paw a crescent.*

Geffrey Elwes Sherif of London, 1607.

ARMS. *Or, a fess azure, surmounted by a bend gules charged with a martlet argent.*

CREST. *Five arrows or, entwined by a snake vert.*

Webling of London Brewer, whose father was a Stranger.

ARMS. *Or, on a chevron sable a ram's head couped argent, on a chief of the second three lozenges or.*

John Dent of London and his wife daughter of — Graunt.

ARMS. *Sable, a fess indented argent, in chief three escallops or; impaling gules, a vine-branch vert fructed argent, surmounted by a bend ermine.*

CREST. *A demi-wolf sable, charged on the neck with a collar dancetté argent.*

Morison of London since altered.

ARMS. *Per saltire or and gules, in pale two leopards' heads of the first, in fess two pelicans of the second, on a chief or, three chaplets gules.*

CREST. *A demi-pegasus or.*

Sr Tho. Fleming Lo. Cheif Justice of England.

ARMS. *Gules, on a chevron between three owls (argent) an ermine spot sable.*

Sr Edw. Coke Lo. Cheif Justice of the Comon Pleas.

ARMS. *Quarterly :—1. Per pale gules and azure, three eagles displayed argent. 2. Argent, a chevron azure between three chaplets gules. 3. Sable, a chevron . . . between three covered cups or. 4. Gules, semé of crosses crosslet fitché, a griffin segreant or.*

Sr Danyell Dun one of the Masters of the requests.

ARMS. *Quarterly :—1 and 4. Azure, a wolf salient and a chief argent. 2. Argent, a lion rampant gules, surmounted by a bendlet sable. 3. Gules, a fess vair, in chief an unicorn passant between two mullets or, a bordure engrailed of the last.* WILKINSON.

Sr William Waade Lieutenant of the Tower.

ARMS. *Quarterly :—1. Azure, a saltire between four escallops or. 2. Or, a chevron between three eagles' heads erased sable. 3. Gules, three garbs or. 4. Azure, two bars argent, on a chief of the last three maunches gules.*

Sr Thomas Edmonds Clark of the Counsell.

ARMS. *Or, a chevron azure, on a canton of the second a fleur-de-lis of the field.*

Sr Thomas Lake Clark of the Signett.

ARMS. *Quarterly :—1 and 4. Sable, on a bend between six crosses crosslet fitché argent, a mullet of the field. 2 and 3. Quarterly argent and sable, on a bend gules three mullets argent, a martlet or for difference.*

Sr Thomas Smythe Clarke of the Counsell.

ARMS. *Azure, a lion rampant or, on a chief argent three torteaux.*

Sr Julius Cesar Chauncellor of the Exchequer.

ARMS. *Quarterly :—1 and 4. Per fess argent and gules, six roses counterchanged. 2. Argent, two bars sable, on a chief of the last three swans argent. 3. Gules, three crescents argent.*

INDEX OF NAMES.

A name in Italics signifies that the arms are blazoned.
„ Capitals „ there is a pedigree given.
„ Brackets is the maiden name.
= signifies "married to a."

INDEX OF PLACES OTHER THAN LONDON MENTIONED IN THIS VISITACION.

FOREIGN PLACES MENTIONED IN THE VISITACION.

WHEN THE *COUNTY ONLY* IS MENTIONED.

Bedfordshire, 70, 81, 84.
Buckinghamshire, 36, 90.
Cambridgeshire, 86.
Cheshire, 88.
Cornwall, 16, 70.
Cumberland, 59, 67.
Derbyshire, 10.
Devonshire, 26.
Durham, 96.
Essex, 4, 9, 10, 31, 43, 45, 46, 47, 57, 61, 74, 79, 94, 96.
Hampshire, 15, 40.
Herefordshire, 35, 40.
Hertfordshire, 17, 36, 61, 84, 87.

Huntingdonshire, 58, 75, 92.
Isle of Wight, 6, 57.
Kent, 5, 22, 38, 45, 50, 53, 73, 82, 90.
Lancashire, 47, 59.
Leicestershire, 33, 71.
Lincolnshire, 11, 21, 23, 24, 26, 43, 66, 75, 87.
Monmouthshire, 87.
Norfolk, 13.
Northamptonshire, 15, 17, 30, 32.
Northumberland, 23, 53.
Oxfordshire, 8.

Shropshire, 4, 25, 28, 35, 39, 70, 94.
Somersetshire, 11, 39, 44.
Staffordshire, 10, 13, 20, 43, 68, 87.
Suffolk, 22, 27, 68.
Surrey, 56.
Sussex, 23, 37, 39, 72, 84, 88.
Warwickshire, 39, 47, 58, 83, 84, 87.
Wiltshire, 21, 68.
Worcestershire, 3, 34.
Yorkshire, 6, 15, 17, 23, 31, 46, 50, 64, 72, 76, 81, 96.

TAYLOR AND CO., PRINTERS,
LITTLE QUEEN STREET, LINCOLN'S INN FIELDS.

PROSPECTIVE PUBLICATIONS.

The Visitation of Leicestershire, in 1619, by Lennard and Vincent.

To be edited by John Fetherston, jun., Esq., F.S.A.

[*In the Press.*

The Visitation of Nottingham in 1614.

To be edited by G. W. Marshall, Esq., L.L.M.

The Visitation of Devonshire in 1620.

To be edited by the Rev. F. Colby, B.D., Fellow of Exeter College, Oxford.

The Visitation of Lincoln.

To be edited by Colonel Chester.

The Visitation of Oxford in 1574 and 1634.

To be edited by W. H. Turner, Esq.

The Visitation of Cornwall in 1620.

The Harleian Society,

INSTITUTED FOR THE

PUBLICATION OF INEDITED MANUSCRIPTS

RELATING TO

GENEALOGY, FAMILY HISTORY, AND HERALDRY.

~~~~~~~~~~~~~~~~~

President.

HIS GRACE THE DUKE OF MANCHESTER.

Vice-Presidents.

THE RIGHT HON. VISCOUNT MIDLETON.
THE RIGHT HON. LORD MONSON.
THE HON. HENRY ROPER-CURZON.
SIR GEORGE F. DUCKETT, BART., F.S.A.
SIR HENRY M. VAVASOUR, BART.
SIR JOSEPH RADCLIFFE, BART.
RALPH ASSHETON, Esq., M.P.
EVELYN PHILIP SHIRLEY, Esq., F.S.A.
R. E. EGERTON-WARBURTON, Esq.

Council.

THE REV. SAMUEL HAYMAN, M.A.
COLONEL JOSEPH LEMUEL CHESTER.
JOHN DAVIDSON, Esq.
SIR JOHN MACLEAN, F.S.A.
WENTWORTH STURGEON, Esq.
JOHN FETHERSTON, Esq., F.S.A.
FAIRLESS BARBER, Esq., F.S.A.
W. AMHURST TYSSEN AMHURST, Esq., F.S.A.
GEORGE W. MARSHALL, Esq., LL.M., F.S.A.
GRANVILLE LEVESON GOWER, Esq., F.S.A.
GEORGE J. ARMYTAGE, Esq., F.S.A., *Hon. Secretary.*
JOSEPH JACKSON HOWARD, Esq., LL.D., F.S.A., *Hon. Treasurer.*

Bankers.

LONDON AND COUNTY, 21, Lombard Street.

Auditors.

J. R. DANIEL-TYSSEN, Esq., F.S.A., 9, Lower Rock Gardens, Brighton.
DUDLEY CARY ELWES, Esq., F.S.A., South Bersted, Bognor.

Rules.

1. This Society shall be called the HARLEIAN SOCIETY.

2. It shall have for its chief object the publication of the Heraldic Visitations of Counties, and any manuscripts relating to genealogy, family history, and heraldry, selected by the Council.

3. The Council shall consist of a President, nine Vice-Presidents, and twelve Members of Council, two of whom shall hold the posts of Secretary and Treasurer; and any four, including the Treasurer or Secretary, shall form a quorum. In case of equality of votes, the Chairman to have a casting vote. Any Candidate may be elected with the consent in writing of one Member of the Council, the Treasurer, and the Secretary.

4. Three Members of the Council shall retire in rotation annually but shall be eligible for re-election.

5. The Annual Subscription shall be One Guinea, paid in advance, and due on the 1st day of January in each year; and Members elected after two hundred and fifty shall have joined, shall pay an Entrance Fee of 10s. 6d. in addition to their first Annual Subscription.

6. The funds raised by the Society shall be expended in publishing such works as are selected by the Council.

7. One volume at least shall be supplied to the Members every year.

8. An Annual Meeting shall be held in the month of June every year, at such time and place as the Council may direct; and due notice shall be sent to the Members of the Society at least a fortnight previously.

9. No work shall be supplied to any Member unless his Subscription for the year be paid; and any member not having paid his subscription for two years, having received notice thereof, shall cease to belong to the Society.

10. The Council may, at their discretion, pay the expense of transcribing from manuscripts whenever two hundred Members, at least, shall have joined the Society; but no payment in money shall be made to any person for editing any work for the Society.

11. No copies of the Publications of the Society shall be supplied to persons not actually Members, and each Member shall be restricted to a single Subscription.

12. An account of the receipts and expenses of the Society to be made up to the 1st of June in each year, and published with a list of the Members and the Rules of the Society in the following volume.

13. These Rules shall not be altered except at the Annual Meeting, and three clear weeks' notice must be given to the Secretary of any such intended alteration.

The Visitation of Devon is now ready, and will be followed by Cumberland. The Visitation of London in 1633–4 is selected for publication in 1873.

Report for the Year 1871–72.

THE Council have pleasure in reporting the steady progress of the Society.

During the past year twenty-five members have joined the Society. Three are dead, Mrs. Baker, Mr. Charles Thurnam, and the Rev. E. Wilton; and five have resigned. The total number on the roll at present is two hundred and eighty-six.

Since the foundation of the Society in 1869, three hundred members have joined, fourteen having died and resigned since then.

During the past year the Society has published 'The Visitations of Nottingham,' by G. W. MARSHALL, Esq., LL.M., F.S.A., and 'The Visitations of Oxford,' by W. H. TURNER, Esq. 'The Visitation of Devon,' edited by the Rev. F. T. COLBY, B.D., F.S.A., is ready. 'The Visitation of Cumberland,' edited by JOHN FETHERSTON, Esq., F.S.A., is in the press. These volumes will comprise the publications for the present year.

The Council have much pleasure in announcing that JOSEPH JACKSON HOWARD, Esq., LL.D., F.S.A., and Colonel JOSEPH LEMUEL CHESTER, have undertaken to edit the valuable 'Visitation of London in 1633, 1634, and 1635,' which has been selected for the publication for next year.

Owing to the importance of this Visitation, embracing as it does many of the pedigrees of the younger branches of the County families, it has been deemed expedient to authorize the illustration of this volume by means of a special fund for the purpose, which has been met by a most hearty response on the part of the members of the Society.

The members can obtain prospectuses by applying to Messrs. TAYLOR and Co., 10, Little Queen Street, High Holborn, for distribution amongst friends.

The Balance-Sheet is appended to this Report, and the Council trust that the members will approve of the Expenditure for the past year.

Harleian Society.

BALANCE SHEET FOR THE YEAR ENDING 31st MAY, 1872.

Dr.

	£	s.	d.
Balance to 31st May, 1871 brought forward	359	7	7
Subscriptions, etc., Entrance Fees	346	2	1
Donations to London Visitation Illustration Fund	98	10	6
	£804	**0**	**2**

Cr.

	£	s.	d.	£	s.	d.
Payments to Messrs. Taylor and Co., for Printing Notts., Orford Visitations, Binding, Circulars, etc.	434	0	4			
Payment on account of Devon Visitation	150	0	0	584	0	4
Woodcuts, Notts. Visitation				10	0	0
Rent of Meeting Room to Midsummer, 1871				5	0	0
Incidental Expenses—						
Honorary Secretary	3	13	6			
Honorary Treasurer	1	3	0	4	16	6
Balance				200	3	4
				£804	**0**	**2**

Examined and found correct by us,

DUDLEY CARY-ELWES.
JOHN R. DANIEL-TYSSEN.

June 6, 1872.

Note—Subscriptions due 1871	£	s.	d.
	6	6	0
,, ,, 1872	89	5	0
	£95	**11**	**0**

JOSEPH JACKSON HOWARD,
Hon. Treasurer.

List of Members,

CORRECTED TO JUNE 1, 1872.

G. Brindley Acworth, F.S.A., Star Hill, Rochester.
Reginald Ames, Cote House, Westbury-on-Trym, Bristol.
W. Amhurst T. Amhurst, F.S.A. (*Council*), Didlington Hall, Brandon.
Frank Andrew, Apsley Place, Ashton-under-Lyne.
Ely Andrew, Mere Bank, Ashton-under-Lyne.
J. E. Andrewes, War Office.
Charles Frederick Angell, F.S.A., Grove Lane, Camberwell, S.E.
The Society of Antiquaries of London, Somerset House, W.C.
William Sumner Appleton, Boston, U.S.A.
Francis R. Armytage, 27, Cambridge Square, W.
George J. Armytage, F.S.A. (*Hon. Secretary*), Clifton, Brighouse.
The Earl of Arran, The Pavilion, Hans Place, S.W.
Ralph Assheton, M.P. (*Vice-President*), Downham Hall, Clitheroe.
John Astley, Broad Gate, Coventry.
W. J. St. Aubyn, 68th Light Infantry, Templemore, Tipperary.
Robert A. C. Godwin-Austen, Chilworth Manor, Guildford.

Lieut.-Colonel Bagnall, Shenstone Moss, near Lichfield.
Charles Baker, F.S.A., 11, Sackville Street, Piccadilly, W.
Fairless Barber, F.S.A. (*Council*), Castle Hill, Rastrick, near Brighouse.
Joseph Gurney Barclay, 54, Lombard Street, E.C.
Thomas H. Bates, Mayfield, Wolsingham.
John Batten, F.S.A., Aldon, Yeovil.
Francis Bayley, 66, Cambridge Terrace, Hyde Park, W.
George Frederick Beaumont, The Knowles, Fixby, Huddersfield.
Robert S. Birkbeck, Anley, Settle.
The Birmingham Library, Union Street, Birmingham. (A. S. Dudley, Librarian).
T. Weld-Blundell, Ince Blundell Hall, Great Crosby, Liverpool.
The Rev. Charles W. Boase, 33, Surrey Street, Strand, W.C.
William Edward Bools, 7, Cornhill, E.C.
Thomas William Boord, F.S.A., 180, Belsize Road, Kilburn, N.W.
Lieut.-Colonel Haworth-Booth, Derwent Bank, Malton, Yorkshire.
W. Consitt Boulter, F.S.A., 6, Park Row, Park Street, Hull.
Lieut.-Colonel John Butler-Bowden, Pleasington Hall, Blackburn.
Edmund M. Boyle, Rockwood, Torquay.
Charles Holte Bracebridge, The Hall, Atherstone, Warwickshire.
The Rev. William Bree, the Rectory, Allesley, Coventry.
The Hon. and Rev. John R. O. Bridgeman, Weston-under-Lyziard, Shifnal.
Thomas Brooke, Armitage Bridge, Huddersfield.
Francis Capper Brooke, Ufford Place, Woodbridge.
The Rev. Frederick Brown, F.S.A., Fern Bank, Beckenham, Kent.
Percy C. S. Bruere, Middleham, Bedale, Yorkshire.
C. G. Prideaux Brune, Prideaux Place, Padstow, Cornwall.
The Rev. Joseph Buckley, M.A., Sopworth Rectory, Chippenham.
Captain W. E. G. Lytton Bulwer, Quebec House, East Dereham.
John Ynyr Burges, Parkanaur, Dungannon, Tyrone, Ireland.
Charles John Burgess, Naval and Military Club, London, W.

SIR BERNARD BURKE, C.B., LL.D., Ulster King-of-Arms, Dublin.
The MARQUIS of BUTE, 83, Eccleston Square, S.W.

BENJAMIN BOND CABBELL, F.R.S., F.S.A., 39, Chapel Street, Edgware Road, W.
F. TEAGUE CANSICK, 28, Jeffrey Street, Kentish Town, N.W.
R. BROWN CANSICK, 2, Bedford Gardens, Kensington, W.
The DOWAGER COUNTESS OF CARNARVON, Pixton Park, Dulverton.
GEORGE ALFRED CARTHEW, F.S.A., East Dereham, Norfolk.
THOMAS CHAPMAN, F.R.S., F.S.A., 25, Bryanstone Square, W.
CHRISTOPHER CHATTOCK, Haye House, Castle Bromwich.
Colonel J. L. CHESTER (*Council*), 16, Linden Villas, Blue Anchor Road, Bermondsey, S.E.
CHETHAM'S LIBRARY, Manchester (Thomas Jones, Esq., Librarian).
Sir ALEXANDER P. BRUCE CHICHESTER, Bart., Arlington Court, Barnstaple.
THOMAS CLOSE, F.S.A., Nottingham.
The Rev. RICHARD CHUTE CODRINGTON, Haygrove, Bridgewater, Somerset.
The Rev. FREDERIC T. COLBY, B.D., F.S.A., Fellow of Exeter College, Oxford.
JAMES EDWIN COLE, Easthorpe Court, Wigtoft, Spalding.
F. S. BERMINGHAM PEN COLE, Freemantle, Southampton.
SYDNEY COLE, Norwood Court, Southall, Middlesex.
JAMES COLEMAN, 22, High Street, Bloomsbury, W.C.
J. KYRLE COLLINS, Wiltondale, Ross, Herefordshire.
JOHN COODE, Polcarm, St. Austell.
WM. HENRY COOKE, Esq., Q.C., F.S.A., 42, Wimpole Street, London.
W. H. COTTELL, 1, Manor Rise, Brixton, S.W.
J. GREGORY COTTINGHAM, Edensor, Chesterfield.
W. PRIDEAUX COURTNEY, Ecclesiastical Commission.
The Rev. H. O. COXE, Bodleian Library, Oxford.
Mrs. JOHN WOODHEAD CROSLAND, Thornton Lodge, Huddersfield.
EDWIN PURVES ROPER-CURZON, Upper Sheen House, Mortlake, S.W.
The Hon. HENRY ROPER-CURZON (*Vice-President*), 47, Argyle Road, Kensington.
The Hon. SIDNEY C. ROPER-CURZON, Upper Sheen House, Mortlake, S.W.

R. S. LONGWORTH DAMES, M.A., 32, Upper Mount Street, Dublin.
C. W. DAVID, Cardiff, Glamorganshire.
JOHN DAVIDSON (*Council*), 14, St. George's Place, Hyde Park Corner, S.W.
ROBERT DAVIES, F.S.A., The Mount, York.
ROBERT DAY, Jun., F.S.A., M.R.I.A., Rockview, Montenotte, Cork.
GORDON DAYMAN, St. Giles's, Oxford.
The Rev. JOHN BATHURST DEANE, M.A., F.S.A., Sion Hill, Bath.
GEORGE DIGBY WINGFIELD DIGBY, Sherborne Castle, Sherborne, Dorsetshire.
Mrs. FETHERSTON DILKE, Maxstoke Castle, Coleshill, Warwickshire.
Sir C. WENTWORTH DILKE, Bart., M.P., 76, Sloane Street, S.W.
ROBERT DOWMAN, 29, Shakspeare Street, Ardwick, Manchester.
HENRY HOLMAN DRAKE, LL.D., Esplanade, Fowey, Cornwall.
Sir GEORGE F. DUCKETT, Bart., F.S.A. (*Vice-President*), Manor House, Bampton. Oxford.
GEORGE F. DUNCOMBE, 17, St. Stephen's Road, Bayswater, W.
ROBERT DYMOND, Bampfylde House, Exeter.

ALBERT EDWARDS, Philadelphia, U.S.A.
J. EDWARDS, M.D., 20, Westmoreland Place, Bayswater, W.
The Rev. HENRY T. ELLACOMBE, M.A., F.S.A., Clyst St. George Rectory, Topsham, Devon.
WILLIAM SMITH ELLIS, Hydecroft, Charlwood, Surrey.
DUDLEY CARY ELWES, F.S.A., South Bersted, Bognor.
V. CARY ELWES, F.S.A., Brigg, Lincolnshire.
WILLIAM ROBERT EMERIS, M.A., F.S.A., Louth, Lincolnshire.

THOMAS FALCONER, one of the Judges of the County Courts, Usk, Monmouthshire.
J. G. FANSHAWE, Board of Trade, Whitehall, S.W.
HENRY MASTER FEILDEN, M.P., Witton Park, Blackburn.
WILLIAM FENNELL, Wakefield.
ROBERT FERGUSON, F.S.A., Morton Hall, Carlisle.
JOHN FETHERSTON, jun., F.S.A. (*Council*), High Street, Warwick.
Lady FETHERSTONHAUGH, Uppark, Petersfield.
W. S. FETHERSTONHAUGH, Rock View, Killucan, Ireland.
GEORGE FITZWILLIAMS, New York, U.S.A.
EDWARD FITZWILLIAMS, Philadelphia, U.S.A.
WILLIAM FLOYD, London Institution, Finsbury Circus, E.C.
CHARLES H. FOX, M.D., The Beeches, Brislington, Bristol.

CLEMENT S. BEST-GARDNER, Eagle's Bush, Neath, Swansea.
JOHN RIBTON GARSTIN, F.S.A., 21, Upper Merrion Street, Dublin.
ARTHUR EDWARD GAYER, Q.C., LL.D., Dublin.
HENRY H. GIBBS, St. Dunstan's, Regent's Park, N.W.
JOSEPH GILLOW, jun., Winckley Square, Preston.
C. GOLDING, 16, Blomfield Terrace, Upper Westbourne Terrace, W.
HENRY GOUGH, 20, Lorn Road, Brixton, S.W.
GRANVILLE LEVESON GOWER, F.S.A. (*Council*), Titsey Park, Godstone.
JAMES GIBSON, Salem, State of New York, U.S.A.
HENRY LEE GRAY, 4, Mont-le-Grand, Heavitree, Exeter.
HENRY SYDNEY GRAZEBROOK, Stourbridge, Worcestershire.
EDWARD GREAVES, M.P., Avonside, Warwick.
BENJAMIN WYATT GREENFIELD, Cranbury Terrace, Southampton.
KELYNGE GREENWAY, Warwick.
The Rev. WILLIAM GRICE, Sherborne House, Lillington, Leamington.
The Rev. HENRY THOMAS GRIFFITH, B.A., Felmingham Vicarage, Norwich.
THOMAS GRISSELL, F.S.A., F.R.S.L., Norbury Park, Mickleham, Dorking.
GORDON GYLL, Remenham House, Wraysbury, Staines.

EDWARD HAILSTONE, F.S.A., Walton Hall, Wakefield.
Sir HENRY ST. JOHN HALFORD, Bart., Wistow, Leicestershire.
The Rev. H. F. HALL, M.A., High Legh, Knutsford, Cheshire.
Sir ROBERT N. C. HAMILTON, Bart., Avoncliffe, Stratford-on-Avon.
Lady FRANCES VERNON-HARCOURT, The Homme, Weobly.
WILLIAM HENRY HART, F.S.A., The Cedars, Overcliff, Rosherville, Kent.
WILLIAM HARVEY, Harrold Hall, Bedford.
The Rev. HENRY HAYMAN, D.D., The School, Rugby.
The Rev. SAMUEL HAYMAN, M.A. (*Council*), The Rectory, Doneraile, Ireland.
Lady HEATHCOTE, Hursley Park, Winchester.
C. PELL HEIGHAM, The Cottage, Bambridge, Winchester.
THOMAS HELSBY, 15, York Chambers, King Street, Manchester.
SPENCER HEREPATH, 18, Upper Phillimore Gardens, W.
WILLIAM PERRY HERRICK, Beaumanor Park, Loughborough, Leicestershire.
Miss FRANCIS MARGERY HEXT, Lostwithiel, Cornwall.
JOHN HIRST, jun., Dobcross, Saddleworth.
The Rev. C. W. HOLBECH, Farnborough, Banbury.
DANIEL DEAN HOPKYNS, F.S.A., Weycliffe, St. Catherine's, near Guildford.
CHANDOS WREN HOSKYNS, M.P., Harewood House, Ross, Herefordshire.
JOSEPH JACKSON HOWARD, LL.D., F.S.A. (*Hon. Treas.*), 3, Dartmouth Row,
    Blackheath, S.E.
HOWMAN, Rev. J. E., Bexwell Rectory, Downham Market.
THOMAS HUGHES, F.S.A., 1, Grove Terrace, Chester.

The INNER TEMPLE LIBRARY, E.C.
The ROYAL IRISH ACADEMY, 19, Dawson Street, Dublin.

The Rev. EDMUND JERMYN, B.A., care of R. F. Jermyn, Esq., 13, Neville Street,
    Onslow Square, S.W.

JOSEPH JONES, Abberley Hall, Stourport.
MORRIS C. JONES, F.S.A., 20, Abercromby Square, Liverpool.
W. STAVENHAGEN JONES, 2, Verulam Buildings, Gray's Inn, W.C.
EDWARD BASIL JUPP, F.S.A., Carpenters' Hall, London Wall, E.C.

The Rev. F. W. KITTERMASTER, All Saints, Coventry.
ARTHUR JOHN KNAPP, Llanforst House, Clifton, Bristol.
T. C. SNEYD KYNNERSLEY, Moor Green, Moseley, Birmingham.

Lieut.-Colonel J. H. BAGOT LANE, King's Bromley Manor, Lichfield.
C. T. LANE, 3, Lombard Court, Lombard Street, E.C.
PHILIP LANGMAN, 7, St. Benet's Place, Gracechurch Street, E.C.
THOMAS LAYTON, F.S.A., Kew Bridge, Middlesex, W.
Sir EDMUND A. LECHMERE, Bart., The Rhydd Court, Upton-on-Severn, Worcester.
The Rev. F. G. LEE, D.C.L., F.S.A., 6, Lambeth Terrace, S.W.
MRS. LITTLEDALE, 19, Queen's Gate Gardens, South Kensington, W.
BEN. LOCKWOOD, Huddersfield.
The Rev. W. J. LOFTIE, 37, Upper Berkeley Street, W.
WILLIAM H. DYER LONGSTAFFE, F.S.A., Gateshead.

Sir JOHN MACLEAN, F.S.A. (*Council*), Pallingswick Lodge, Hammersmith, W.
SILVANUS J. MACY, 189, Front Street, New York, U.S.A.
The Rev. A. R. MADDISON, Friskney, Boston, Lincolnshire.
G. BUCKLEY MATHEW, H.B.M. Minister Plenipotentiary, Rio de Janeiro.
C. H. MALLOCK, Cockington Court, Torquay.
The DUKE OF MANCHESTER (*President*), 1, Great Stanhope Street, W.
GEORGE W. MARSHALL, LL.M., F.S.A. (*Council*), Weacombe House, Bicknoller, Taunton.
BERNULF DE CLEGG MATTINSON, Oldham.
WALTER C. METCALFE, Epping, Essex.
The Right Hon. VISCOUNT MIDLETON, Peper Harrow Park, Godalming.
Lieut.-Colonel MILLER, R.A., Woolwich, S.E.
MINNESOTA HISTORICAL SOCIETY, St. Paul, Minnesota, U.S.A.
The Rev. JOHN MIREHOUSE, Colsterworth, Grantham.
Captain R. MOLESWORTH, High Legh, Knutsford.
The Right Hon. LORD MONSON (*Vice-President*), Gatton Park, Reigate.
THOMAS H. MONTGOMERY, 400, Walnut Street, Philadelphia, U.S.A.
Lieut.-Col. CHARLES THOMAS JOHN MOORE, F.S.A., Frampton Hall, near Boston.
FREDERICK J. MORRELL, St. Giles', Oxford.
EDWARD MORTON, F.S.A., The Bank, Malton, Yorkshire.
GEORGE J. MURRAY, Hartford House, Werneth, Oldham.
C. R. SCOTT-MURRAY, Danesfield, Great Marlow.

C. N. NEWDEGATE, M.P., Arbury Hall, Nuneaton, Warwickshire.
Miss NEWMAN, 6, Patshull Road, Kentish Town, N.W.
Miss CHARLOTTE NEWMAN, 6, Patshull Road, Kentish Town, N.W.
JAMES NEWMAN, 235, High Holborn, W.C.
Captain W. NEWSOME, R.E., Gravesend.
J. W. NICHOLL-CARNE, D.C.L., St. Donat's Castle, Bridgend, Glamorganshire.
JOHN GOUGH NICHOLS, F.S.A., 25, Parliament Street, S.W.
Colonel SIDNEY NORTH, M.P., Wroxton Abbey, Banbury.

WILLIAM JOHN O'DONNAVAN, LL.D., M.R.I.A., Foxcroft House, Portarlington.
EVAN ORTNER, 3, St. James's Street, S.W.
FREDERIC OUVRY, F.S.A., 12, Queen Anne Street, Cavendish Square, W.

The Rev. THOMAS DOUGLAS PAGE, Pembroke College, Oxford.

Sir CHARLES J. PALMER, Bart., Dorney Court, Windsor.
The Rev. FIELDING PALMER, Eastcliff, Chepstow.
The Rev. GEORGE PALMER, F.S.A., 53, Lowndes Square, S.W.
The Rev. JOHN PAPILLON, M.A., F.S.A., Lexdon Rectory, Colchester.
The Rev. J. T. PARKINSON, D.C.L., F.S.A., Ravendale, Grimsby.
DANIEL PARSONS, Stuarts Lodge, Malvern.
D. WILLIAMS PATERSON, Newark Valley, New York, U.S.A.
EDWARD PEACOCK, F.S.A., Bottesford Manor, Brigg, Lincolnshire.
Rev. A. J. PEARMAN, Rainham Vicarage, Sittingbourne.
CHARLES GEORGE PERCEVAL, Passenham Manor, Stony Stratford.
IRA B. PECK, Woonsocket, Rhode Island, U.S.A.
HENRY PECKETT, Carlton Husthwaite, Thirsk, Yorkshire.
THOMAS A. PERRY, Bitham House, Leamington.
GEORGE PLUCKNETT, F.S.A., Manor House, Finchley, N.
LEMUEL POPE, Concord, Massachusetts, U.S.A.

Sir JOSEPH RADCLIFFE, Bart. (*Vice-President*), Rudding Park, Wetherby.
The Rev. CANON RAINE, York.
J. R. RAINES, Burton Pidsea, Hull.
SAMUEL RIGBY, Bruch Hall, Warrington.
ALEXANDER RIVINGTON, 27, Cleveland Gardens, Hyde Park, W.
The Rev. C. J. ROBINSON, M.A., Norton Canon Vicarage, Weobly.
The Rev. EDWARD ROGERS, M.A., Blachford, Ivy Bridge, Devon.
R. R. COXWELL-ROGERS, F.S.A., Dowdeswell Court, Andoversford, Gloucester.
The Rev. ROBERT ROE ROGERS, 104, Exmouth Street, Parkfield Terrace, Birken-
head.
The ROYAL LIBRARY, Windsor Castle.
The Rev. DAVID ROYCE, The Vicarage, Lower Swell, Stow-on-the-Wold.
JAMES RUSBY, 21, Ainger Terrace, Regent's Park, N.W.
The DUKE OF RUTLAND, K.G., Belvoir Castle, Grantham.
J. PAUL RYLANDS, Highfield, Thelwall, Warrington.

EVELYN PHILIP SHIRLEY, F.S.A. (*Vice-President*), Lower Eatington Park, Strat-
ford-on-Avon.
ROBERT HARDISTY SKAIFE, The Mount, York.
Rev. E. H. MAINWARING SLADEN, M.A., F.R.G.S., Alton Berners, Marlborough.
J. S. SMALLFIELD, 32, University Street, W.C.
The Rev. WALTER SNEYD, Keele Hall, Newcastle, Staffordshire.
CHARLES SOTHERAN, 6, Meadow Street, Moss Side, Manchester.
CHARLES STEWART, The West Hall, High Legh, Knutsford.
THOMAS STEWARDSON, Germantown, Philadelphia, U.S.A.
WENTWORTH STURGEON (*Council*), 11, King's Bench Walk, Temple, E.C.
JOHN SYKES, M.D., F.S.A., Doncaster.

The Rev. JAMES TAYLOR, Brigham by Carlisle.
Miss CAROLINE C. THAYER, Boston, U.S.A.
SAMUEL VASPER THOMAS, Newborough, Wimborne, Dorset.
THOMAS THOMSON, M.D., Clarence Terrace, Leamington.
ROBERT F. TOMES, Weston, Stratford-on-Avon.
T. G. TOMKINS, Great Ouseburn, York.
GEORGE D. TOMLINSON, Huddersfield.
HENRY TREHERNE, Latymer House, Brook Green, W.
Sir J. SALUSBURY TRELAWNY, Bart., M.P., Trelawne, Liskeard, Cornwall.
Sir WALTER C. TREVELYAN, Wallington, Newcastle-on-Tyne
JOSEPH HERBERT TRITTON, 54, Lombard Street, E.C.
GEORGE TUCK, New Road, Windsor.
WILLIAM HENRY TURNER, 8, Turl Street, Oxford.
The Rev. SAMUEL BLOIS TURNER, F.S.A., South Elmham, Halesworth, Suffolk.
PHILIP TWELLS, M.A., Chase Side House, Enfield.
J. R. DANIEL TYSSEN, F.S.A., 9, Lower Rock Gardens, Brighton.
Sir HENRY M. VAVASOUR, Bart. (*Vice-President*), Holton Hall, Halesworth.

Benj. Llewelyn Vawdrey, Tushington Hall, Whitchurch, Salop.
Colonel Vivian, Rose Hill, Camborne, Cornwall.

Edward Waltham, Walcombe House, Stockwell Green, London, S.W.
R. E. Egerton-Warburton (*Vice-President*), Arley Hall, Northwich.
The Earl of Warwick, Warwick Castle, Warwick.
Edmond Chester Waters, Upton Park, Poole.
Frank G. Watney, 17, Pembridge Crescent, Bayswater, W.
John Watney, jun., F.R.G.S., F.S.A., 16, London Street, Fenchurch Street, E.C.
The Rev. James Webb, M.A., The Parsonage, Hartshead, Normanton.
Archibald Weir, M.D., St. Mungho's, Great Malvern.
Lieut.-Colonel Weston, Hunterstone House, West Kilbride, Ayrshire.
William H. Whitmore, Boston, U.S.A.
The Rev. Thomas Whorwood, D.D., Vicar of Willoughby, near Rugby.
Miss Williams, Orchard Wyndham, Taunton.
The Rev. Augustin Williams, Icomb Rectory, Stow-on-the-Wold.
Francis Willington, Tamworth, Warwickshire.
The Hon. Robert C. Winthrop, Boston, United States.
John Withem, 9, Pall Mall East, S.W.
R. H. Wood, F.S.A., Crumpsall, Manchester.
Charles H. L. Woodd, F.G.S., Roslyn, Hampstead, N.W.
Ashbel Woodward, M.D , Franklin, Connecticut, U.S.A.
Richard Woof, F.S.A., F.R.S.L., Guildhall, Worcester.
W. H. Wright, Philadelphia, U.S.A.
William W. E. Wynne, F.S.A., Peniarth, Towyn, Merioneth.